T0123400

Debunking
Christian Zionism
—— and ——
Evolutionary Creation

Debunking Christian Zionism —— and —— Evolutionary Creation

Two Bible-Based Essays for Evangelicals

LES NASSERDEN

WESTBOW
P R E S S®
A DIVISION OF THOMAS NELSON
& ZONDERVAN

WestBow Press books may be ordered through booksellers or by contacting:

WestBow Press
A Division of Thomas Nelson & Zondervan
1663 Liberty Drive
Bloomington, IN 47403
www.westbowpress.com
1 (866) 928-1240

Because of the dynamic nature of the Internet, any web addresses or links contained in
this book may have changed since publication and may no longer be valid. The views
expressed in this work are solely those of the author and do not necessarily reflect the
views of the publisher, and the publisher hereby disclaims any responsibility for them.

Any people depicted in stock imagery provided by Getty Images are
models, and such images are being used for illustrative purposes only.
Certain stock imagery © Getty Images.

This book is a work of non-fiction. Unless otherwise noted, the author and the publisher
make no explicit guarantees as to the accuracy of the information contained in this book
and in some cases, names of people and places have been altered to protect their privacy.

Scripture quotations are taken from The Holy Bible, New International
Version®, NIV® Copyright © 1973, 1978, 1984, 2011 by Biblica,
Inc.® Used by permission. All rights reserved worldwide.

ISBN: 978-1-9736-5611-1 (sc)
ISBN: 978-1-9736-5612-8 (hc)
ISBN: 978-1-9736-5610-4 (e)

Library of Congress Control Number: 2019902700

Print information available on the last page.

WestBow Press rev. date: 3/13/2019

When Will Evangelicals, Including Pentecostals, Admit They Were Wrong on Israel?

Christians Do *Not* Have a "Biblical
Mandate" to Support Modern Zionism

A LOT OF EVANGELICAL AND PENTECOSTAL CHRISTIANS passionately or passively believe they should support the modern state of Israel. I have many friends in this category. These Christian Zionists believe the establishment and existence of modern Israel is a fulfillment of biblical prophecy, and they believe they have a biblical mandate to support the Jews as they return to and rule their ancient homeland. Some historical prominent leaders of this movement have been Hal Lindsey, the late Jerry Falwell, Pat Robertson, John Hagee, Tim LaHaye, John MacArthur, and Benny Hinn, not to mention many other historical and contemporary evangelical and Pentecostal Christian leaders, theologians, ministries, and organizations. In 2004, Timothy

P. Weber wrote a book about the movement entitled *On the Road to Armageddon: How Evangelicals Became Israel's Best Friend.*

I too, both as a layperson and a pastor, adopted this Christian Zionist conviction, not so much because it was a thoughtful, deliberate choice but because it was an entrenched sentiment in the evangelical/Pentecostal circles with which I was associated.

I now strongly believe Christians should *not* believe modern Israel is a direct fulfillment of biblical prophecy, and I believe Christians do *not* have a biblical mandate to support the modern state of Israel. I also believe that working through this issue will clarify one's understanding of the Christian gospel. It is not that I am against Israel but that I want to be true to the Judeo-Christian scriptures. Lastly, I keep asking myself, "When will evangelicals, including Pentecostals, admit they were wrong on Israel?"

There are four main reasons why I disagree with Christian Zionists.

First, Christian Zionists emphasize the Abrahamic covenant and its land clause but fail to tell you how the later Mosaic covenant augments, or sets conditions on, the former covenant and clause. Thus, the only people who ever had a

God-given right to the ancient land of Israel were covenant-keeping believers.

Second, Christian Zionists emphasize the numerous Old Testament prophecies about the restoration of Israel but fail to tell you that these prophecies are always associated with an eschatological Messianic kingdom of covenant belief. Since there is not one Old Testament prophecy that explicitly says God will restore Israel to its homeland in unbelief (as modern Israel has been for seventy years), it is presumptuous to think that the establishment and expansion of Israel in 1948 and 1967 were direct fulfillments of prophecy.

Third, Christian Zionists emphasize that they adhere to basic evangelical Christian doctrine but fail to tell you everything the New Testament says about the Messiah—Jesus Christ. More specifically, Christian Zionists fail to tell you that Jesus Christ supremely fulfilled the earlier covenants God made with Abraham, Moses, and David and that, as the absolutely perfect embodiment of Israel's faith, he forever redefined Israel. In other words, you cannot talk about true Israel without talking about Israel's Messiah and Eternal King—Jesus Christ.

Fourth, Christian Zionists emphasize political and practical aid to modern Israel, oftentimes making such aid a litmus test on one's love and commitment to God. But they fail to tell you what the New Testament says about Jewish nationalism and Christian ministerial priorities. Instead of an agenda of unbiblical racism, politicism, and militarism, the Christian church should be emphasizing love, prayer, evangelism, discipleship, and the ministry of the Holy Spirit for all people—Jews and Gentiles alike.

Now we will look at these four reasons or points in more detail.

Point #1. The Old Testament Abrahamic covenant cannot be isolated from the Mosaic covenant and other subsequent divine covenants. (Christian Zionism isolates the Abrahamic covenant.)

Christian Zionists virtually always use the Abrahamic covenant, which dates back to approximately 1900 BCE, as the basis of their theology promoting the return to, and rule of, ancient Israelite land by contemporary Jews. The specific content of the Abrahamic covenant is first mentioned in Genesis 12:1–3 (New International Version).

> The LORD had said to Abram, "Leave your country, your people and your father's household and go to the land I will show you. I will make you into a great nation and I will bless you; I will make your name great,

and you will be a blessing. I will bless those who bless you, and whoever curses you I will curse; and all peoples on earth will be blessed through you."

In total, God spoke to Abraham about this covenant on at least seven occasions spanning a period of more than thirty years (Gen. 12:1, 12:7, 13:14, 15:1, 17:1, 18:17, and 22:15). Thus, the threefold promise that God made to Abraham had to do with a special land (i.e., Canaan), a great posterity (i.e., many descendants), and a divine blessing for the whole world. All three of these promises, which are commonly believed to comprise the Abrahamic covenant, are collectively mentioned to Abraham on two occasions (Gen. 12:1 and 22:15). They are collectively repeated to both Abraham's son Isaac (Gen. 26:2–5) and Isaac's son Jacob (Gen. 28:12–15). It should be noted that the third aforementioned promise of the Abrahamic covenant (the one having to do with a blessing for the whole world) is mentioned five times in Genesis (see 18:18) and is climactic in relation to the first two promises.

A few things need to be highlighted about this Abrahamic covenant. In Genesis 17, when God confirmed the covenant to Abraham, the word "everlasting" is repeatedly used for the covenant in general (vv. 7, 19), the land promise stretching eastward to the Euphrates River (v. 8), and the sign of the covenant (i.e., male physical circumcision) (v. 13).

The meaning of the Hebrew word *olam,* translated as "everlasting," "forever," or "eternal" (NIV), is similar to its English equivalent in that it can refer to either a long time or infinity. In Genesis 21:33, the word is used in the Hebrew term *El Olam,* which means "the Everlasting God" or "the Eternal God." The same Hebrew word is used, referring to the land promise, in Genesis 13:15, 48:4, Exodus 32:13, and Joshua 14:9. King David also used the word olam to describe the Abrahamic covenant in Psalm 105:10.

Christian Zionists often emphasize this everlasting characteristic of the Abrahamic covenant but usually do not tell you that the word olam is also frequently used to describe various temporary aspects of the subsequent Mosaic covenant, such as the Feast of Unleavened Bread (Exod. 12:24), the Day of Atonement (Lev. 16:34), the showbread of the tabernacle (Lev. 24:8), and the priesthood of Phinehas and his descendants (Num. 25:13). Consequently, the Abrahamic covenant was everlasting in some sense—you could say unconditional—but it was also conditional. In other words, the Abrahamic covenant could be broken by individuals, as Genesis 17:14 attests: "Any uncircumcised male, who has not been circumcised in the flesh, will be cut off from his people, he has broken my covenant."

It is also relevant that, centuries later, God got angry and was going to administer capital punishment because one of Moses's Midian-born sons was not circumcised (Exod. 4:24–26). So the point that will keep resurfacing is that the (Abrahamic) covenant was enacted by God through Abraham's descendants in a long-term (everlasting) sense, but it was always conditional in a short-term (individual) sense. Faith and obedience were always preeminent in God's relationship with Abraham and his descendants. More specifically, there is an expressed strong emphasis on faith and obedience in five of the seven occasions God spoke to Abraham about the covenant (Gen. 12:4, 15:6, 17:1, 18:19, 22:15–18). Abraham's faith and obedience were also emphasized by God to Isaac in Genesis 26:5. So not only could the covenant be broken by neglecting circumcision, but it is strongly inferred that the covenant could be broken by faithlessness and disobedience. After all, circumcision was the "sign" of the covenant. As a physical symbol, circumcision signified faith and obedience toward God and ownership by God. The sign was not greater than the covenant it represented.

The fact that foreigners could enter the covenant relationship (Gen. 17:12–13, 27) also indicates that the covenant transcended a purely physical/ethnic relationship. Thus foreigners (Gentiles) were later allowed to participate in the Passover celebration—but only if they were circumcised (Exod. 12:43–49). Yes, the primary locus of the Abrahamic covenant was Abraham's physical/ethnic descendants of promise through Isaac (i.e., those who believed and obeyed

God as Abraham did). But the covenant was never restricted to them.

Not only were both Isaac and Jacob mindful of the threefold promissory (Abrahamic) covenant, and specifically the Canaan land promise, but later Hebrews in the days of Joseph and his brothers were also mindful of the same land promise as revealed in Genesis 48:3 and 50:24. Still later, after four hundred years of Egyptian bondage, God's subsequent revelation to Moses was clearly a continuation or augmentation of the former (Abrahamic) covenant, as the following exemplary scripture reveals. Exodus 6:2–5, 8 reads,

> God also said to Moses, "I am the LORD. I appeared to Abraham, to Isaac and to Jacob as God Almighty, but by my name the LORD I did not make myself known to them. I also established my covenant with them to give them the land of Canaan, where they lived as aliens. Moreover, I have heard the groaning of the Israelites, whom the Egyptians are enslaving, and I have remembered my covenant … And I will bring you to the land I swore with uplifted hand to give to Abraham, to Isaac and to Jacob. I will give it to you as a possession. I am the LORD."

You could also read Exodus 3:16 and Exodus 13:5, 11. As the preceding scriptures in the book of Exodus indicate, the deliverance of Israel from Egypt, under Moses's leadership, approximately five hundred years after Abraham, was clearly a partial fulfillment of God's covenant commitment to Abraham, Isaac, and Jacob, to give them the land of Canaan.

The (Mosaic) covenant was formally given to Moses and the Israelites by God at Mount Sinai within the first year after the exodus from Egypt, and it is explicitly referred to in Exodus chapters 19, 24, and 34. The many requirements and ramifications of this very conditional covenant are continuously stipulated in the Old Testament books of Exodus through Deuteronomy. Thus the incipient moral and ceremonial requirements associated with the former Abrahamic covenant, pertaining to faith/obedience and circumcision/altar worship, are enlarged and elaborated in the later Mosaic covenant. Hence the moral requirements of the Mosaic covenant have to do with the Ten Commandments plus many other commands, while the ceremonial requirements of the same covenant have to do with the tabernacle and the sacrificial system.

So the Abrahamic and Mosaic covenants are related in terms of human requirements. In other words, God chose to reveal his (moral and ceremonial) will or covenant requirements in stages. Theologians call this "progressive revelation." I realize

9

the "moral" and "ceremonial" distinctions are arbitrary, but they do show how these two covenants are related. The Abrahamic and Mosaic covenants are also related in terms of purpose. Both covenants, with the human requirement to believe and obey, were progressive means toward an end, the end being a closer relationship with God. This grand purpose can be summed up in the clause, or its equivalent, "I will be your God, and you will be my people." This clause, or its equivalent, is invariably associated with the concept of divine covenant. Pertaining to the Abrahamic covenant, Genesis 17:7–8 reads, "I will establish my covenant as an everlasting covenant between me and you and your descendants after you for the generations to come, to be your God and the God of your descendants after you. The whole land of Canaan, where you are now an alien, I will give as an everlasting possession to you and your descendants after you; and I will be their God."

Pertaining to the Mosaic covenant, Exodus 6:7 reads, "I will take you as my own people, and I will be your God," while Leviticus 26:12 reads, "I will walk among you and be your God, and you will be my people." (See also Exod. 19:5f and Deut. 29:12f) So, the point that needs to be repeated is that the Abrahamic and Mosaic covenants are related in terms of requirements (i.e., they both stress faith and obedience for God's moral and ceremonial will), and they are also related in terms of purpose (i.e., they both are progressive means for a closer relationship with God).

The book of Deuteronomy was the second giving of the Mosaic law or covenant, while the Israelites were in Moab on the east side of the Jordan River. As the previous generation of Israelites had died in the wilderness (Num. 14:21–35; Deut. 1:35), it was important for the covenant law to be expounded to the new generation before they entered the Promised Land (Deut. 29:1). The emphasis on blessings for obedience and curses for disobedience in Deuteronomy chapters 27 through 31, and Joshua 8:30–35, also testify to the conditional nature of the Mosaic covenant, as does the repetitive use in Deuteronomy of the dire word and theme "remember" (e.g., 4:9–10, 23; 5:15; 8:2, 11; 9:7; 24:9; 32:7). The implication, if you do not remember, is that there are serious consequences. That being said, we often overlook another key word and theme in Deuteronomy, that being "land". The word *land* is used more than one hundred times in Deuteronomy, specifically referring to the future home of Israel, and in some twenty-five of these times the word is associated with "Abraham, Isaac, and Jacob" or "your (fore)fathers" (e.g., 1:8, 6:10, 7:12, 10:11, 19:8, 26:3, 30:20, 34:4). Consequently, like the earlier land claim references in Exodus, the land claim of Deuteronomy and the Mosaic covenant is, without a doubt, one and the same as the land claim of Genesis and the Abrahamic covenant. Thus it must be restated that the

Abrahamic/Mosaic land covenant is enacted by God to and through Israel in an everlasting long-term sense but is always conditional and temporary in a short-term sense.

The subsequent history of Israel, starting with the days (and biblical book) of Joshua, confirms the truth and seriousness of the conditional short-term sense. God's supernatural sustenance and blessing of the people and land of Israel was often limited, if not removed, due to faithlessness and disobedience, as the remaining books of the Old Testament reveal. This faithlessness and disobedience culminated in the Assyrian captivity of the ten northern tribes, referred to as Israel, in 722 BCE, and the Babylonian captivity of the two southern tribes, referred to as Judah, between 605 and 586 BCE. The Israelites, or Jews, never totally recovered from these divine disciplines, although they were later allowed to live and worship in their homeland under foreign rule.

What I am saying is that the Abrahamic/Mosaic land covenant had everything to do with Israel's faith and obedience and God's supernatural sustenance and blessing. From the birth of Isaac, to the deliverance from Egypt, to the provisions in the wilderness, to the conquering of Canaan, et cetera, the spectacular supernatural power of God was manifest throughout in response to faith and obedience in God's progressively revealed (covenant) will and law. Without faith and obedience and the supernatural power of God, both the people and land of Israel were helpless and hopeless, and under God's severe disciplinary judgment.

I am absolutely amazed that Lindsey, Falwell, Robertson, Hagee, LaHaye, MacArthur, Hinn, and company ignore the relationship between the Abrahamic and Mosaic covenants pertaining to the land of Israel. When Christian Zionists focus on the Abrahamic covenant, and not this Mosaic augmentation, they have adopted an incomplete, expedient, and erroneous theology. Similarly, when Christian Zionists incessantly recite the Abrahamic clause, "I will bless those who bless you, and those who curse you I will curse," and thus give defacto unqualified support to Zionism, they effectively ignore the Mosaic injunction whereby God sometimes curses as well as blesses Abraham's physical descendants (see Deut. chap. 28). The use of this Abrahamic clause by Christian Zionists is clearly a case of taking scripture out of context.

It should also be noted that this clause in Genesis 12:1ff—"I will bless those who bless you, and those who curse you I will curse"—is not specifically referred to anywhere in subsequent Old Testament scripture, and there is only one allusion to this clause in the New Testament, that being Zechariah's prophecy about Jesus recorded in Luke 1:71–74. Yet Christian Zionists continue to highlight this clause. Undoubtedly, this clause was proven true on numerous occasions in Israelite history prior to the Assyrian (722 BCE) and Babylonian (586

BCE) captivities, not to mention during and after the later captivity of Judah, but how applicable or effective the clause has been for the Jews during the last two thousand years (since the new covenant) is theologically and historically dubious indeed.

Another Old Testament example of both everlastingness and conditionality that is relevant to our discussion is the Davidic covenant recorded in 2 Samuel chapter 7. While King David wanted to build a "house" (i.e., a temple) for God, God reversed the order and decided to build a "house" (i.e., an everlasting dynasty and kingdom) for King David. This divine promise was given in approximately 1000 BCE, nearly a thousand years after the Abrahamic covenant, and a few hundred years after the Mosaic covenant.

This prophetic message from God to David via Nathan had three usages of the Hebrew word olam, meaning "everlasting" or "forever" (2 Sam. 7:13, 16), and David's responsive prayer had five such usages (2 Sam. 7:24–26, 29). Near the end of his life, David used the same word, olam, as he reflected on this "everlasting covenant" (2 Sam. 23:5). At the same time, there are scriptures that indicate this Davidic covenant was somewhat conditional—that is, there is an "if" clause that stresses faith and obedience as found in 2 Samuel 7:14f; 1 Kings 2:4, 8:25, 9:4f; Psalms 89:30–32 and 132:11f. 1 Kings

9:4ff, for example, recording God's words to King Solomon after the temple was built, reads,

> As for you, if you walk before me in integrity of heart and uprightness, as David your father did, and do all I command and observe my decrees and laws, I will establish your royal throne over Israel forever, as I promised David your father when I said, "You shall never fail to have a man on the throne of Israel." But if you or your sons turn away from me and do not observe the commands and decrees I have given you and go off to serve other gods and worship them, then I will cut off Israel from the land I have given them and will reject this temple I have consecrated for my Name. Israel will then become a byword and an object of ridicule among all peoples.

Thus the dichotomous nature of the Davidic covenant, whereby it is both everlasting and conditional, should not surprise us, as the Abrahamic covenant was the same. What is surprising or alarming is that Christian Zionists will recognize how the Davidic covenant (i.e., the Messianic king and kingdom) augments the worldwide blessing clause of the Abrahamic covenant, but they will not recognize how the Mosaic covenant (i.e., the specified moral conditions) augments the land clause of the Abrahamic covenant. Strictly from an Old Testament perspective, the only constituency of people who had and have a God-given right to the ancient land of Israel were and are faithful and obedient (covenant-keeping) Jews.

It is now necessary that we briefly consider the Old Testament literary or canonical prophets. This group is also known as the "latter" prophets, who along with the "former" prophets (i.e., Joshua, Judges, Samuel, and Kings) comprise the second section of the Hebrew scriptures, hence the traditional classification "the Law, the Prophets, and the Writings." Included in the literary prophets are Isaiah, Jeremiah, Ezekiel, Hosea, Joel, Amos, Obadiah, Jonah, Micah, Nahum, Habakkuk, Zephaniah, Haggai, Zechariah, and Malachi. Although the Old Testament book of Daniel is formally included in the third group of scripture (i.e., the Writings), we, like the Greek Septuagint and English arrangements, will consider it as being prophetic in nature. Keep in mind that these sixteen prophets lived and ministered between approximately 850 and 400 BCE, thus after the Abrahamic, Mosaic, and Davidic covenants. Consequently, these spokesmen for God were interpreters or commentators of Old Testament covenant religion. The first thing that must be noted about these literary prophets is that the word and name Abraham is mentioned only seven times in all their messages—four times in Isaiah, and once apiece in Jeremiah,

Ezekiel, and Micah. That is not a lot of references, considering there is a sum of 245 so-called chapters in the corpus of Old Testament prophetic literature.

Furthermore, these God-inspired prophets never explicitly refer to the specific covenant associated with Abraham. Contemporary Christian Zionists should take note of that pertinent fact. Moreover, apart from the first five books of the Old Testament, or in other words, after the Mosaic covenant was instituted, the Abrahamic covenant is explicitly referred to a mere four times in all the remaining Old Testament books (i.e., 2 Kings 13:23; 1 Chron. 16:16; Neh. 9:7–8; and Ps. 105:9). Surely, the Old Testament former and latter (literary) "Prophets," and "the Writings," indicate that the Abrahamic covenant must not be unduly interpreted or elevated into something it is not.

The fact is that the literary prophets had a composite concept of the Abrahamic, Mosaic, and Davidic covenants. I use the word *composite* here to mean that various individual parts make up the whole. You do not find these prophets singling out any of the three previous covenants. Rather the literary prophets understood these three smaller previous covenants were closely related and together formed a bigger, all-encompassing covenant.

They also foresaw a future kingdom when this covenant would be finalized or consummated. Thus all three of the primary topics addressed by the literary prophets (i.e., true righteousness, divine judgment, and God's future kingdom) were inherent in each of the previous divine covenants. More specifically, when these prophets spoke or wrote about true righteousness, they were exhorting their fellow Israelites to be "circumcised in their hearts" in accordance with the requirements of the Abrahamic (Gen. 15:6), Mosaic (Deut. 10:16), and Davidic (1 Kings 2:3f) covenants. Likewise, when these prophets spoke or wrote about divine judgment, they were warning their fellow Israelites of the dreadful consequences of faithlessness and disobedience as revealed in the Abrahamic (Gen. 17:14), Mosaic (Deut. 28:15ff), and Davidic (2 Sam. 7:16) covenants.

And finally, when these prophets spoke or wrote about God's future kingdom, they were comforting their fellow Israelites by looking forward to that which the Abrahamic (Gen. 12:3c), Mosaic (Deut. 18:14ff), and Davidic (2 Sam. 7:16) covenants anticipated. Lastly, the following scripture— Ezekiel 37:24b–26a—is most revealing in terms of the composite/consummated concept of divine covenant. Note how this futuristic scripture alludes to all three previous divine covenants, plus the forthcoming new covenant:

They will follow my laws and be careful to keep my decrees (an allusion to the Mosaic covenant). They will live in the land I gave to my servant Jacob, the land where your fathers lived. They and their children and their children's children will live there forever (an allusion to the Abrahamic covenant), and David my servant will be their prince forever (an allusion to the Davidic covenant). I will make a covenant of peace with them; it will be an everlasting covenant (an allusion to the new covenant) (my parentheses).

So the point is that, contrary to contemporary Christian Zionist theology, the literary prophets of old never isolated the Abrahamic covenant. The testimony of these prophets confirms that the Abrahamic covenant was always perceived in conjunction with God's subsequent covenant revelations. This composite concept of covenant also explains why in the Old Testament the Hebrew word for covenant (*berith*) is always singular and never plural.

Point #2. The Old Testament prophetic "Restoration of Israel" has to do with an eschatological Messianic kingdom of belief. (Christian Zionism has to do with a temporal nation of unbelief.)

The issue and debate about the restoration of Israel revolves around a multifaceted question: What did the word and concept *Israel* refer to (a) originally in the Pentateuch (i.e., the first five books of the Old Testament), (b) later in the Old Testament, especially in the literary prophets, and (c) still later in the apostolic New Testament? This point #2 will be restricted to the above (a) and (b) subpoints. The New Testament criteria, subpoint (c), will be examined in points #3 and #4. To begin with, it must be reiterated that God's intention and interest in Abraham had to do with more than just external features (i.e., land, descendants, and circumcision). Rather, God wanted to have a close relationship with people, and he thus initiated a covenant plan starting with Abraham.

As was previously explained in our discussion of point #1, the core of this divine covenant with Abraham had to do with faith and obedience. Abraham's son, Isaac, and grandson, Jacob, proved to be faithful and obedient to God, and in Genesis chapter 32, God changed Jacob's name to Israel because Jacob "struggled with God and men and have overcome" (v. 28). Surely this change of name reveals something about the volitional nature of being in a covenant relationship with God. In other words, such a relationship requires persevering faith and obedience. The twelve sons of Israel subsequently became the foundation of the Israelite nation. Remember that foreigners could become participants in this infant covenant-keeping nation (Gen. 17:12–13, 23, 27), and that circumcision was the crucial but symbolic "sign" of the covenant with God (Gen. 17:11). From the beginning, Israelite identity and destiny were centered in faith and obedience toward God's unfolding covenant Word, rather than land, ethnicity, and ritual.

The preeminence of faith and obedience in the covenant with Abraham and his descendants was continued in the so-called Mosaic covenant. It was crucial that the Israelites believe and obey God's further holy requirements revealed to and through Moses. If you look up the words *cut off* and *death* in a biblical concordance (i.e., a study book that lists all the words in the Bible), you will find that, in the Pentateuch, there are several sins or violations of the covenant that got people "cut off" from Israel or that required the death penalty. Similarly, if you look up the words *unclean* and *defile* in a biblical concordance, you will find that, in the Pentateuch, many acts and conditions resulted in uncleanliness and defilement, which in turn temporarily estranged people from their God and their community. The point is that in the Pentateuch, Israel was synonymous with holiness and covenant law.

If one did not adhere to certain divine requirements, they were exterminated or excluded from Israel. At Mount Sinai, God said to Moses and the Israelites, "Now if you obey me fully and keep my covenant, then out of all nations you will be my treasured possession. Although the whole earth is mine, you will be for me a kingdom of priests and a holy nation" (Exod. 19:5f). The Hebrew word for holy means "set apart." Thus this word is frequently used in the Pentateuch for anything, anyplace, or anyone set apart for God's special purposes. As the preceding scripture (i.e., Exod. 19:5f) indicates, the nation of Israel was set apart and holy when it fully believed and obeyed the divine covenant. So Israel was more than just the physical descendants of Abraham, Isaac, and Jacob. Most fundamentally, Israel was the covenant-keeping people of God.

A biblical concordance also reveals that native-born Israelites and "aliens" (i.e., covenant-keeping foreigners) were often given the same status in this holy nation. More specifically, aliens within the Israelite community could celebrate the Passover (Exod. 12:48f), aliens were required to keep the Sabbath (Exod. 20:10), aliens participated in and were beneficiaries of the annual Day of Atonement ceremony (Lev. 16:29f), aliens could offer burnt offerings or sacrifices (Lev. 17:8ff), aliens were to obey God's commands about sexual behavior (Lev. 18:26), aliens had the same laws and penalties for blasphemy, murder, et cetera (Lev. 24:10ff), aliens could celebrate the various God-ordained feasts (Deut. 16:9–17), and aliens within the Israelite community were expected to know and obey the (Mosaic) law of God (Deut. 31:12). In other words, all these responsibilities and privileges meant that covenant-keeping aliens were essentially the people of God—Israelites. This biblical evidence indicates that faith and obedience were of supreme importance to the God that created and sustained Israel. Finally, the dire warnings of expulsion from the (promised) land for covenant disobedience, as revealed in Leviticus chapter 26 and Deuteronomy chapters 28–30, also indicate that Israelite identity and destiny were centered in faith and obedience toward God, rather than in land, ancestry, or circumcision rite.

Did the Old Testament literary prophets uphold this emphasis on faith and obedience among the Israelite nation? Absolutely. We have already noted how faith and obedience were at the core of the prior Abrahamic, Mosaic, and Davidic covenants, and we have also noted that true righteousness was a primary topic of these literary prophets. They continually stressed the letter and spirit of the Mosaic covenant law. As a matter of fact, *all* sixteen literary prophets championed true righteousness (i.e., faith and obedience).

These sixteen prophets reveal that the sin-prone Israelites continually needed correction and encouragement before, during, and after the (Babylonian) exile. Directly related to true righteousness (or the lack of it) is the second primary topic of the literary prophets, that being "divine judgment." Of the thirteen preexilic and exilic literary prophets, ten spoke and wrote about the divine judgment of Israel/Judah. Although Obadiah, Jonah, and Nahum did not discuss the topic, the ten prophets who did speak and write about the divine judgment of Israel/Judah did so largely based on the Mosaic covenant law as found in Leviticus chapter 26 and Deuteronomy chapters 28–30. The exilic statesman and prophet Daniel sums up the prophetic viewpoint concerning Israel/Judah in his prayerful confession recorded in Daniel 9:8–14.

This brings us to the crux of the literary prophets. Most of what these prophets spoke and wrote about anticipates or pertains to either (a) the exile of the ten-tribe northern kingdom (Israel) to Assyria in 722 BCE, or (b) the exile of the two-tribe southern kingdom (Judah) to Babylon in 605–586 BCE. These exiles played a major role in the history of Israel, and these exiles had everything to do with the divine covenant. Apart from Obadiah, Jonah, Nahum, and Zephaniah, the remaining seven preexilic literary prophets all specifically predicted exile for Israel/Judah.

This list includes Joel, Hosea, Amos, Isaiah, Micah, Jeremiah, and Habakkuk. These prophets bluntly and unapologetically declared that God would sovereignly destroy most of Israel/Judah because of flagrant faithlessness and disobedience to the divine covenant. The prophet Hosea relayed the following divine message to the northern kingdom of Israel: "you are not my people, and I am not your God" (Hosea 1:9). Historians and scholars refer to the "ten lost tribes of Israel" (i.e., the ones conquered by and deported throughout Assyria), but history and scholarship know virtually nothing about these tribes. Suffice it to say that in these two exiles, many Israelites died, many Israelites were forcibly moved, and many (but not all) Israelites were assimilated into foreign nations.

What do these exiles to Assyria and Babylon say or imply about Israel? Surely, the main thing these exiles reveal is the seriousness and life/death consequences of the divine covenant to which Israel was a party. The blatant sin of those in northern Israel and southern Judah caused God to both abandon and destroy most of his so-called people. The alarming words of God's prophets (e.g., Hosea 1:9; Amos 9:1ff; Jer. 11:1ff; Ezek. 2), and the relentless actions of God's sovereign agents (i.e., the Assyrians and Babylonians), indicate that blatant sinners were not God's people. As God revealed to Abraham in Genesis 15:7–21, and later reminded the Israelites in Deuteronomy 28:26 and Jeremiah 34:18–20, if you continually break the divine covenant, you can expect your dead body or carcass to be eaten by birds and animals. So God's discipline or judgment of the Israelites could be severe.

At the same time, Jeremiah had predicted that the exile to Babylon would last only seventy years (Jer. 25:11f, 29:10), as the Israelites were still chosen or elected by God to fulfill God's plan of salvation for the world. As some have said, Israel was divinely elected to be the "delivery system" for the Messiah. Also, the fact remains that there was always a remnant of faithful and obedient Israelites, plus the fact that the literary prophets spoke and wrote about the "restoration of Israel" that was beyond judgment and exile. So God was not finished with the entity called Israel. This brings us to the third primary topic of the literary prophets, that being God's future kingdom or the restoration of Israel.

Twelve of the sixteen literary prophets spoke and wrote about the restoration of Israel. These prophetic references were very significant and prominent, as they provided comfort and hope in the midst of warning and judgment. The literary prophets who did not refer to the future restoration of Israel were Jonah and Nahum, who addressed the Assyrians in Ninevah; Habakkuk, who discussed the Babylonians; and postexilic Malachi, who preached about true righteousness and divine judgment. Of the twelve literary prophets who did refer to the restoration of Israel, eight ministered in the two and a half centuries before the exiles (i.e., Obadiah, Joel, Amos, Hosea, Isaiah, Micah, Zephaniah, and Jeremiah), two ministered during the Babylonian exile (Daniel and Ezekiel), and two ministered during a brief period after the Babylonian exile (Haggai and Zechariah). Following is a list of the main references to the restoration of Israel among the literary prophets.

Obadiah: verses 15–21

Joel: chapter 3

Amos: chapter 9:11–15

Hosea: chapters 2:14–23, 3:5

Isaiah: chapters 2:1–5, 4, 9, 10:20–22, 11, 12, 24, 25, 26, 27, 49, 54, 55, 65:17–25

Micah: chapters 4, 5, 7:8–20

Zephaniah: chapter 3:8–20

Jeremiah: chapters 16:14f, 23:1–8, 30, 31, 32, 33

Daniel: chapters 2, 7, 9, 10, 11, 12

Ezekiel: chapters 34, 36, 37, 39:25–29

Haggai: chapter 2:6–9, 20–23

Zechariah: chapters 2, 8, 9, 10, 12, 13, 14

The "restoration of Israel" in the Old Testament has got to be one of the most neglected topics of biblical study. If you study the preceding scriptures, you will find five dominant characteristics.

First, the restoration of Israel is an eschatological event that happens at the end of God's plan for this world. There are references or allusions to this characteristic among all twelve noted prophets. Two examples follow. Amos 9:15 says, "I will plant Israel in their own land, never again to be uprooted from the land I have given them, says the LORD your God." Ezekiel 37:25 says, "They will live in the land I gave to my servant Jacob, the land where your fathers lived. They and their children and their children's children will live there forever, and David my servant will be their prince forever." Two other examples are Micah 4:1 and Daniel 7:27.

Second, the restoration of Israel follows some drastic divine judgments upon the nations of the world. Ten of the noted twelve prophets refer or allude to these judgments. Two examples follow. Obadiah 15 says, "The day of the LORD is near for all nations. As you have done, it will be done to you; your deeds will return upon your own head." Zephaniah 3:8 says, "I have decided to assemble the nations, to gather the kingdoms and to pour out my wrath on them—all my fierce anger. The whole world will be consumed by the fire of my jealous anger." Two other examples are Joel 3:2 and Haggai 2:22.

Third, the restoration of Israel is marked by righteousness and covenant relationship. Ten of the twelve noted prophets refer or allude to this characteristic. Two examples follow.

Micah 4:2 says, "Many nations will come and say, 'Come, let us go up to the mountain of the LORD, to the house of the God of Jacob. He will teach us his ways, so that we may walk in his paths.' The law will go out from Zion, the word of the LORD from Jerusalem." Jeremiah 32:40 says, "I will make an everlasting covenant with them: I will never stop doing good to them, and I will inspire them to fear me, so that they will never turn away from me." Two other examples are Zephaniah 3:9 and Ezekiel 34:25.

Fourth, the restoration of Israel has to do with a Davidic king and kingdom. Five or six of the twelve noted prophets refer to a Davidic king (Hag. 2:23 may be viewed as questionable). Two examples follow. Ezekiel 37:24 says, "My servant David will be king over them, and they will all have one shepherd. They will follow my laws and be careful to keep my decrees." Hosea 3:5 says, "Afterward the Israelites will return and seek the LORD their God and David their king. They will come trembling to the LORD and to his blessings in the last days." Two other examples are Amos 9:11 and Jeremiah 33:15.

Fifth, the restoration of Israel is based in the historic land of Israel, including Jerusalem. Nine of the twelve noted prophets refer or allude to this characteristic. Two examples follow. Joel 3:20 says, "Judah will be inhabited forever and Jerusalem through all generations." Isaiah 27:12f says, "In that day the LORD will thresh from the flowing Euphrates to the Wadi of Egypt, and you, O Israelites, will be gathered up one by one. And in that day a great trumpet will sound. Those who were perishing in Assyria and those who were exiled in Egypt will come and worship the LORD on the holy mountain in Jerusalem." Two other examples are Obadiah 20 and Zechariah 14:1ff.

The present author readily admits that all the preceding (and succeeding) scriptural references should be read and studied in context. When this is done, the emerging consensus of the literary prophets concerning the restoration of Israel is remarkable indeed, and the aforementioned five characteristics are indisputable.

These five characteristics of the prophetic restoration of Israel need to be restated:

1. It is an eschatological event that happens at the end of God's plan for this world.

2. It follows some drastic divine judgments upon the nations of the world.

3. It is marked by righteousness and covenant relationship.

4. It has to do with a Davidic king and kingdom.

5. It is based in the historic land of Israel, including Jerusalem.

The question remains, "Who is Israel?" In other words, who were the twelve literary prophets (and God who was inspiring them) referring to when they spoke and wrote about the restoration of Israel? Christian Zionists are insistent that these prophets were prophesying about the physical descendants of Abraham, Isaac, and Jacob (i.e., Jewish people), who come into an eschatological covenant relationship with the Davidic Messiah. After all, the word Israel, throughout the Old Testament, is associated with the people, land, and kingdom of the physical descendants of Abraham, Isaac, and Jacob. Thus Christian Zionists insist that their viewpoint or theology is consistent with a historical-grammatical literal interpretation of scripture. But is the Christian Zionist viewpoint as consistent as it initially appears? I do not think so.

To begin with, the divine covenant with Abraham (Gen. chap. 12) came before the changing of Jacob's name to Israel (Gen. chap. 32). And the third divine promise of the covenant with Abraham had to do with a blessing for the whole world through Abraham's descendants. So God's focus, from the beginning of His interaction with Abraham, was on the covenant and the whole world. As the prophet Isaiah much later indicated, the nation of Israel was God's "servant" to implement His covenant plan for the world (e.g., Isa. 41:8–9, 44:1–2, 21). This divine covenant plan was to enable sinful human beings (Jews and Gentiles) to be reconciled to a holy

God. The Old Testament reveals that this divine covenant plan combined the smaller Abrahamic, Mosaic, and Davidic covenants, and anticipated a final, consummated covenant centered around a Davidic king—the Messiah. Isaiah refers to this final covenant as "my covenant of peace" (54:10) and "an everlasting covenant" (55:3). Jeremiah refers to this final covenant as "a new covenant" (31:31) and "an everlasting covenant (32:40). And Ezekiel refers to this final covenant as "a covenant of peace (34:25, 37:26) and "an everlasting covenant" (37:26).

The point is that all of these "covenant" references by Isaiah, Jeremiah, and Ezekiel had to do with an eschatological event that happens at the end of God's plan for this world. In other words, all of these "covenant" references pertain to the restoration of Israel. Clearly, the literary prophets did not foresee the difference between the "suffering servant" inaugural coming of the Davidic king and kingdom and the "glorious savior" eschatological coming of the same Davidic king and kingdom. Looking from the distant past, it simply appeared to these prophets that the Davidic king and kingdom would come once. Thus most of what the literary prophets spoke and wrote about had to do with the climactic second coming of the Davidic king, which they thought of as "the restoration of Israel." David (e.g., Ps. 22), Isaiah (e.g., Isa. 52:13, 53:12), Micah (Mic. 5:2), and Jeremiah (e.g., Jer. 31:31ff), among others, were divinely enabled to glimpse certain aspects of the inaugural or first coming of the Davidic king and kingdom.

The prophet Isaiah was also divinely enabled to foresee another significant feature of the coming Davidic kingdom—that is, the inclusion of the Gentiles. Once again, the context of Isaiah's words about the inclusion of the Gentiles was often that of the eschatological Davidic king and kingdom, or in other words, the restoration of Israel. Following is a list of Isaiah's references to the inclusion of the Gentiles: 2:2–4; 11:10; 18:7; 24:14–16; 25:6–8; 42:6; 49:6, 22; 55:5; 56:1ff; 60:3; 66:18ff. Isaiah 42:6c, which is yet another allusion to the Davidic "servant" king, says, "I will keep you and will make you to be a covenant for the people and a light for the Gentiles." Isaiah 49:6, which also appears to be a reference to the same king, says, "It is too small a thing for you to be my servant to restore the tribes of Jacob and bring back those of Israel I have kept. I will also make you a light for the Gentiles, that you may bring my salvation to the ends of the earth."

Isaiah 56:1–8 clearly says God accepts "foreigners" and "eunuchs" who are righteous—that is, those who are faithful and obedient. Verse eight of this scripture says, "The Sovereign LORD declares—he who gathers the exiles of Israel: 'I will gather still others to them besides those already gathered.'" Thus the preceding scriptures indicate that Gentiles will be included in the eschatological restoration of Israel.

When Christian Zionists say the restoration of Israel has to do with national ethnic Israel, they are espousing an erroneous doctrine. They do not understand how the Abrahamic, Mosaic, Davidic, and final (new) covenants are integrally related. They also downplay the emphasis of faith and obedience in God's covenant plan, and they ignore the testimony of the literary prophets. And finally, Christian Zionists, believe it or not, underappreciate the concept of the Messiah.

The Old Testament has several references, allusions, and foretellers of the Messiah. The coming "prophet" that Moses wrote about in Deuteronomy 18:14–19 refers to the Messiah and His prophetic ministry. David, in Psalm 110:4, refers to the ancient priest of God Melchizedek, mentioned in Genesis 14:18–20, as one who foretells the priestly ministry of the kingly Messiah. And then there are the kingly references to the Messiah in the literary prophets (e.g., Isa. 9:7; Jeremiah 23:5; Ezek. 34:24). Thus the Old Testament says the coming Messiah is going to be a prophet, a priest, and a king.

As we have already noted, the Messiah was also referred to as a "servant." It is interesting that Isaiah referred to both the corporate nation of Israel (e.g., 41:8ff, 42:18ff), and the individual Messiah of Israel (e.g., 42:1ff, 49:1ff), with the title "servant." The point is that the Messiah encapsulated or embodied everything that Israel was ever meant to be. The

Messiah was the apex, even the epitome, of Israel. This cannot be overemphasized. The coming kingdom that Abraham, Moses, David, and the literary prophets (including Daniel) anticipated totally revolved around the Messiah.

The analysis of this point #2 has been purposely restricted to Old Testament criteria. These criteria show the prophetic restoration of Israel revolves around the Messiah and His consummate covenant. Christian Zionists err when they think these Old Testament criteria support or endorse the restoration or establishment of the modern state of Israel in and after 1948 CE. Modern Israel does not have the first four of the five needed aforementioned characteristics to be equated with the prophetic restoration of Israel. For example, modern Israel is temporal—not eschatological, secular—not righteous, and constitutional—not monarchial.

Another inferred characteristic of the prophetic restoration of Israel, as depicted in the vision of Ezekiel 37:1–14, is that it involves the resurrection of dead people. The vision of the countless dry bones coming to life is not about modern Israel being physically and spiritually restored, as Christian Zionists erroneously suppose. Rather this vision is about the ultimate resurrection of all previously dead covenant-believing Israelites (which includes covenant-believing Gentiles). As the adjacent scriptures in Ezekiel (i.e., chap. 34, 36, and 37:15–28) confirm, this vision is about the prophetic restoration of Israel explained earlier. Of course, honest Christian Zionists admit these discrepancies, but then they arbitrarily readjust their theology and say modern Israel is a "harbinger" of restored Israel. A harbinger is something that is preliminary to, foreruns, or heralds, the future. In other words, Christian Zionists believe the founding of modern, secular Israel is a crucial first link in the chain of prophetic eschatological events.

I believe this "harbinger" tactic is completely expedient, is based on sentimentalism, and ignores the current theological point. This point #2 is a plea for evangelical/Pentecostal Christians to study more closely what the Old Testament says about (a) the covenantal nature of Israel's divine calling, (b) the eschatological/Messianic/righteous nature of the prophetic restoration of Israel, and (c) the role and ramifications of Israel's Messiah. Lastly, the aforementioned fifth characteristic, pertaining to the historic land of Israel and city of Jerusalem, does not necessarily mean the restoration of Israel is an exclusive temporal Jewish entity. Rather this fifth characteristic simply states where the restoration of Israel will be based during the millennium and/or on the restored earth in the final age.

Due to the "earthly" descriptions of the restoration of Israel portrayed in the Old Testament literary prophets, and the "earthly" descriptions related to Gog and Magog in Ezekiel chapters 38 and 39 (and Rev. chap. 20), I do not adhere to the idea that the holy land and holy city were old covenant types that were completely fulfilled in the holy Messiah or Christ. Temporal Jerusalem and vicinity definitely appears to play a part in the end-times scenario relating to the millennium. The few additional Jewish references, among the same restoration of Israel prophecies, pertaining to a temple, sacrifices, and the Feast of Tabernacles (e.g., Jer. 33:17f; Dan. 9:27; Zech. 14:16ff), plus the temple vision of Ezekiel chapters 40 through 48, may be literal or typological, but either way they do not negate the rationale and substance of this point #2. My personal conviction and conclusion is that I cannot allow these few ambiguous Jewish references (which may very well be typological), and which are totally ignored by the New Testament writers, to override the overwhelming bulk of Old Testament criteria relative to the restoration of Israel.

Point #3. The New Testament teaches that the Messiah (Jesus Christ) supremely fulfills the Israelite faith of the Old Testament. (Christian Zionism downplays the role and ramifications of the Messiah.)

The New Testament says (a) Jesus of Nazareth was the long-awaited Messiah (Hebrew) or Christ (Greek), which means "anointed one," and (b) this Jesus Christ inaugurated the "new covenant" that Jeremiah (31:31ff) and others foresaw. As the Messiah, Jesus was the perfect Israelite. His ancestors and parents were Israelites (i.e., Jewish). His upbringing and life experiences were Jewish. He essentially lived his whole life in the historic land of Israel, and his three-year public ministry was primarily in and to Israel. For example, Jesus Christ said, "I was sent only to the lost sheep of Israel" (Matt. 15:24). But he was more than just another outstanding Jew or Israelite. He was conceived by the Holy Spirit (Luke 1:35), and his birth (Matt. 1; Luke 1–2), circumcision (Luke 2:21ff), and youth (Matt. 2:1ff; Luke 2:41ff), were marked by some strange events.

When he was thirty years old, and John the Baptist refused to baptize him, Jesus replied, "Let it be so now, it is proper for us to do this to fulfill all righteousness" (Matt. 3:15). These words to John the Baptist hinted at something more strange about Jesus—his sinlessness, which he later claimed (John 8:46). Furthermore, John the Baptist saw "the Spirit of God descending like a dove and lighting on him" (Matt. 3:16), and then John heard a voice from heaven saying, "This is my Son, whom I love; with him I am well pleased" (Matt. 3:17).

The next three years were the most remarkable three years in recorded history. This man Jesus went about healing people of every disease imaginable, casting out all kinds of demons from people, and teaching extensively and authoritatively about godly truth and human relations. The common people were attracted to him, and the Jewish religious leaders were jolted, amazed, perplexed, and often angered at him. He spoke like a prophet and was perceived by many to be one. He spoke of faith and obedience. He also spoke about sin, forgiveness, sacrifice, and death, even his own death. He was not afraid of anyone, and had such self-assurance. He was in total command of his surroundings. The natural world, whether water, wind, bread, or fish, obeyed him. He talked about Abraham's children, Moses's law, and David's psalms.

He went further. He said he was before Abraham (John 8:58). He said he came to fulfill the law of Moses (Matt. 5:17). And he did not rebuke the people when they proclaimed him "Son of David" and treated him like a king (Matt. 21: 9, 15f). He even agreed with Peter when the disciple replied, "You are the Christ, the Son of the living God" (Matt. 16:16). On several occasions, he also claimed to be one with God the Father (e.g., John 14:1ff, 17:1ff). And he capped it all off by saying, "All authority in heaven and on earth has been given to me" (Matt. 28:18).

But the strangest of things that this Jesus did was to allow the Jewish and Roman authorities, and many people in concert, to kill him on a cross. It was as if he was a lamb to be slaughtered. He just passively let them kill him, without resisting at all. And then another strange thing happened. Reports started spreading that several people, even many people, claimed he had risen from the dead and was alive.

These people, his followers, started saying this Jesus Christ died for the sin of the world—that is, to take upon himself sin in all its fullness. The claim that this Jesus Christ rose from the dead was said to be the crux of everything he said and did. Either he rose from the dead, and thus vindicated his claim to be the Christ/Messiah—the Son of God—who conquered sin and death, or he stayed dead and with him all his untrue words. The New Testament repeatedly says Jesus did in fact rise from the dead and will someday conclusively prove to be the glorious "King of Kings and Lord of Lords" (Rev. 19:16).

As Israel's Messiah, this man Jesus embodied the absolute perfect Israelite. His importance cannot be overemphasized. He fulfilled the Abrahamic covenant—that is, the third divine promise to Abraham about a worldwide blessing (John 8:56; Acts 3:24f; Gal. 3:8). He fulfilled the Mosaic covenant by completely obeying the "Law," and by being a sinless high priest and perfect sacrifice (John 8:46; Heb. 7:26f). And he fulfilled the Davidic covenant by being the descendant of King David who inaugurated an everlasting kingdom (Luke 1:32f; Matt. 21:1–16; John 18:36f). Likewise, Jesus met the "Davidic king" requirement of the eschatological "restoration of Israel" mentioned by some of the Old Testament prophets. In sum, the New Testament says Jesus was the ultimate in terms of being a prophet, a priest, and a king, and that he supremely fulfilled the Abrahamic, Mosaic, Davidic, and

New covenants. The crux of this point #3 is this: Everything that Israel ever was or was ever meant to be was fulfilled by Jesus Christ. To say that Jesus Christ did not redefine Israel is to deny New Testament Christology.

Let us now look at how Jesus Christ is related to the Old Testament prophetic "restoration of Israel" (point #2). To begin with, Jesus's forerunner, John the Baptist, appeared with the message: "Repent, for the kingdom of heaven is near" (Matt. 3:2). Jesus started his own ministry with the same message: "Repent, for the kingdom of heaven is near" (Matt. 4:17). Mark 1:15 records Jesus's words: "The time has come. The kingdom of God is near. Repent and believe the good news." Similarly, Luke 4:43 records Jesus's words: "I must preach the good news of the kingdom of God to the other towns also, because that is why I was sent." John 3:3 records Jesus's words to Nicodemus: "I tell you the truth, no one can see the kingdom of God unless he is born again." A concordance reveals over one hundred references to the "kingdom" of heaven/God in the gospels of Matthew, Mark, and Luke (John has five such references). Clearly, the kingdom of God was a central teaching of Jesus's ministry, and I might add that the New Testament book of Acts also has several specific references to the "kingdom of God" (i.e., Acts 8:12; 14:22; 19:8; 20:25; 28:23, 31).

It is also relevant that Jesus taught that the kingdom of God was both a present reality and a future realm. Consider the following four examples by Jesus that, when read in context, all refer to the "present" aspect of the kingdom of God.

1. "From the days of John the Baptist until now, the kingdom of heaven has been forcefully advancing, and forceful men lay hold of it" (Matt. 11:12).

2. "But if I drive out demons by the Spirit of God, then the kingdom of God has come upon you" (Matt. 12:28).

3. "When Jesus had called the Twelve together, he gave them power and authority to drive out all demons and to cure diseases, and he sent them out to preach the kingdom of God and to heal the sick" (Luke 9:1f).

4. "Once having been asked by the Pharisees when the kingdom of God would come, Jesus replied, 'The kingdom of God does not come with your careful observation, nor will people say, Here it is, or There it is, because the kingdom of God is within/among you'" (Luke 17:20f).

Now consider another four examples by Jesus that, when read in context, all refer to the "future" aspect of the kingdom of God.

1. "Once again, the kingdom of heaven is like a net that was let down into the lake and caught all kinds of fish. When it was full, the fishermen pulled it up on the shore. Then they sat down and collected the good fish in baskets, but threw the bad away. This is how it will be at the end of the age. The angels will come and separate the wicked from the righteous" (Matt. 13:47ff).

2. "I tell you the truth, I will not drink again of the fruit of the vine until that day when I drink it anew in the kingdom of God" (Mark 14:25).

3. "There will be weeping there, and gnashing of teeth, when you see Abraham, Isaac, and Jacob and all the prophets in the kingdom of God, but you yourselves thrown out. People will come from east and west and north and south, and will take their places at the feast in the kingdom of God" (Luke 13:28f).

4. "While they were listening to this, he went on to tell them a parable, because he was near Jerusalem and the people thought that the kingdom of God was going to appear at once. He said, 'A man of noble birth went to a distant country to have himself appointed king and then to return. So he called ten of his servants and gave them ten minas. Put this money to work, he said, until I come back.'" (Luke 19:11ff).

The implication of this last recited scripture (i.e., parable), if you did not understand it, is that there is still a period of time, with accompanying responsibilities, before the expected kingdom of God (represented by the appointed king) comes or returns. In summary, the most basic characteristic of both the present and future aspects of the kingdom of God is divine rulership. A kingdom requires a king who rules, and over and over again in the New Testament, the man Jesus is implicated as the divine king. Thus the kingdom of God is a present spiritual reality for those who, by faith and obedience, allow Jesus Christ to be the king and ruler of their lives in this age, and it is these people (along with those from Old Testament days who had faith and obedience) who will be allowed to enter the future kingdom of God in the age to come where Jesus Christ is the eternal king and ruler.

The point is that the future kingdom of God in the New Testament, most notably in the first three Gospels, is extremely similar to the Old Testament restoration of Israel. Granted, it took Jesus's disciples a while to link the future kingdom of God that Jesus talked about with the restoration of Israel that the Old Testament prophets talked about. When two confused disciples were unknowingly talking with Jesus after his resurrection on the road to Emmaus, they commented, "But we had hoped that he was the one who was going to redeem Israel" (Luke 24:21). A short time later, Jesus's disciples posed the question, "Lord, are you at this time going to restore the kingdom to Israel?" (Acts 1:6). These two preceding scriptures show that the disciples were still expecting the Lord's imminent kingdom to be a national entity.

Finally, Peter and the disciples understood the connection between the restoration of Israel and the future kingdom of God. Referring to Jesus, Peter said, "He must remain in heaven until the time comes for God to restore everything, as he promised long ago through his holy prophets" (Acts 3:21). Christian Zionists need to ponder this statement by Peter about Jesus, and they thus need to admit that the future kingdom of God is synonymous with the prophetic restoration of Israel. Keep in mind that Jesus never specifically said anything about "the restoration of Israel," or about ethnic/national Israel being restored to their homeland. When Christian Zionists say the "fig tree" of Matthew 24:32 is an intentional symbol of national Israel, this is a clear case of "eisegesis" (i.e., reading something into the text that is not there).

Rather Jesus uses the fig tree analogy to show that just as tender twigs and new leaves indicate that summer is near, the list of signs in Matthew 24 will someday indicate that Jesus's second coming is near. Like Jesus, the apostles and New Testament writers never subsequently refer to "the restoration of Israel," nor do they ever mention that the

Jewish people still had a divine right to their homeland or that Jewish possession of their homeland would someday be important. For example, I think it is very significant that the writer of the book of Hebrews in the New Testament says, "For he (Abraham) was looking forward to the city with foundations, whose architect and builder is God ... Instead, they were longing for a better country—a heavenly one. Therefore God is not ashamed to be called their God, for he has prepared a city for them" (Heb. 11:10, 16).

It should also be noted that although Jesus did not address the topic of the millennium, the return of the "KING OF KINGS AND LORD OF LORDS," and the ushering in of the thousand-year reign of Jesus Christ, as depicted in Revelation chapters 19–20, plus the "new heaven," "new earth," and "new Jerusalem" scenario of Revelation chapter 21, all align quite well with the aforementioned five characteristics of the prophetic restoration of Israel.

Point #4. The New Testament prioritizes Christian ministry (i.e., love, prayer, evangelism, discipleship, and the ministry of the Holy Spirit) for all nations. (Christian Zionism prioritizes practical, political, and military aid for one nation.)

We have already noted how God, in Old Testament Israelite times, was concerned about non-Jews (i.e., Gentiles). We noted the climactic third (worldwide blessing) promise of the Abrahamic covenant, then the provisions in both the Abrahamic and Mosaic covenants for "alien" participation, and then the inclusion of the Gentiles in several of Isaiah's prophecies about the future restored kingdom. Granted, we also noted how Jesus Christ was Israel's Messiah, and how his earthly life and ministry focused on the historic nation of Israel. After all, Jesus did say, "I was sent only to the lost sheep of Israel" (Matt. 15:24).

But there is more to the story, if you know what I mean. Jesus also said, "I have other sheep that are not of this sheep pen. I must bring them also. They too will listen to my voice, and there shall be one flock and one shepherd" (John 10:16). These other sheep are Gentiles. It should be noted that Jesus also forecasted the destruction of the Jewish temple and the city of Jerusalem, as recorded in the gospels of Matthew (ch. 24), Mark (ch. 13), and Luke (ch. 21). Jesus said this impending destruction was God's sovereign judgment of the Jews for not recognizing the Messiah and the new covenant (Luke 19:41–44; 21:20–24). This destruction of the temple and city took place later in 70 CE and 135 CE, at the hands of the Romans.

Two examples in the ministry of Jesus further reveal his sympathy for Gentiles. The first example is when Jesus honored the faith of a Gentile centurion in Capernaum by healing the centurion's paralyzed and suffering servant (Matt.

8:5ff). Jesus's remarks at the time are significant: "I tell you the truth, I have not found anyone in Israel with such great faith. I say to you that many will come from the east and the west, and will take their places at the feast with Abraham, Isaac and Jacob in the kingdom of heaven. But the subjects of the kingdom will be thrown outside into the darkness, where there will be weeping and gnashing of teeth." Jesus knew that some Gentiles from distant lands would have faith in the God of Israel and thus enter the future kingdom of God, and Jesus also knew that some "subjects of the kingdom" (i.e., Jews) would not have such a faith and future, on the contrary. The second example is when Jesus honored the faith of a Gentile woman in Syrian Phoenicia by casting out a demon from the woman's daughter (Mark 7:24ff).

Again, the exchange between Jesus and the Gentile is insinuating. When the woman made her desperate request, Jesus responded, "First let the children eat all they want, for it is not right to take the children's bread and toss it to their dogs," to which the woman replied, "Yes Lord, but even the dogs under the table eat the children's crumbs." Jesus concluded the exchange by saying, "For such a reply, you may go; the demon has left your daughter." Jesus knew the good news of the kingdom of God was ultimately not just for the people of Israel but for all people.

This awareness of Gentile inclusion was also expressed in some of Jesus's teachings. In both the parable of the wedding banquet (Matt. 22:1ff), and the parable of the great banquet (Luke 14:15ff), the servants of the host are told to go out and gather others (meaning Gentiles) and bring them to the banquet, even though they were not initially invited. The incipient international characteristic of Jesus's ministry culminated with him saying, "go and make disciples of all nations" (Matt. 28:19), and "be my witnesses in Jerusalem, and in all Judea and Samaria, and to the ends of the earth" (Acts 1:8).

The remaining New Testament outlines the development of the early Christian church as it spread into Gentile lands. This development started with (a) the conversion of the apostle Paul in Acts chapter 9, of whom the Lord Jesus said, "This man is my chosen instrument to carry my name before the Gentiles and their kings" (v. 15), and (b) the vision of the apostle Peter in Acts chapters 10 and 11, whereby the Spirit of Jesus made it clear that God accepted believing Gentiles. Perhaps the greatest repository of truth regarding the theology and ministry of the Christian church, as it relates specifically to Jews and Gentiles, is the corpus of letters in the New Testament by the apostle Paul.

Notwithstanding the ad hoc nature of these thirteen letters, whereby they were written to specific local churches and leaders for specific circumstances, five of these letters explicitly refer to the intrinsic equality of believing Jews and Gentiles within the Christian church (i.e., Rom. 1:16, 3:9, 10:12; 1 Cor. 12:12f; Gal. 3:26–29; Eph. 2:11–3:6; and Col. 3:9–11). Thus a main theme of Paul's life and letters is "justification by faith" (in Jesus Christ) for both Jews and Gentiles.

Consider the letter or book of Romans. Paul wrote this letter in about 58 CE to the predominantly Gentile Christian church in Rome. As I just made reference to, this theological treatise makes the following three statements.

1. Romans 1:16 reads: "For I am not ashamed of the gospel, because it is the power of God that brings salvation to everyone who believes: first to the Jew, then for the Gentile."

2. Romans 3:9c reads: "For we have already made the charge that Jews and Gentiles alike are all under the power of sin."

3. Romans 10:12 reads: "For there is no difference between Jew and Gentile—the same Lord is Lord of all and richly blesses all who call on him."

Of course, one cannot adequately discuss the theology and ministry of the Christian church in relation to Jews and Gentiles without considering Romans chapters 9–11. Admittedly, the following comments on these chapters are best understood with an open Bible at hand and a concentrated focus. The reason that parts of these three chapters are somewhat analyzed here is because Christian Zionists heavily depend upon a certain interpretation of some of the latter verses in chapter 11. These specific verses are as follows: "Israel has experienced a hardening in part until the full number of the Gentiles has come in. And in this way all Israel will be saved" (Rom. 11:25b, 26a NIV). Thus Christian Zionists are adamant that the latter "Israel" in verse 26a refers to the same ethnic Israel mentioned earlier in verse 25b.

So, sometime in the future, according to Christian Zionist interpretation, there will be a mass conversion of ethnic Israelites to saving faith in Jesus Christ. And this scripture and futuristic scenario is largely why Christian Zionists are predisposed to support the modern state of Israel. But there is a huge contextual problem with this Christian Zionist interpretation, plus some related grammatical problems.

The huge problem for Christian Zionists is that nowhere in Romans chapters 9–11, including verses 25 and 26 of the latter chapter, is Paul talking about the (eschatological) future, on the contrary. At the beginning of each of these three chapters, Paul is talking about the present time (i.e., the first century of the common era) as he elucidates the enduring unbelief (in Jesus Christ) of most Israelites.

In chapter 9 he says, "I have great sorrow and unceasing anguish in my heart. For I could wish that I myself were cursed and cut off from Christ for the sake of my brothers, those of my own race, the people of Israel" (9:2–4). In chapter 10, he says, "Brothers, my heart's desire and prayer to God for the Israelites is that they may be saved" (10:1). In chapter 11, he says, "I ask then: Did God reject his people? By no means! I am an Israelite myself, a descendant of Abraham, from the tribe of Benjamin" (11:1). It must be repeated that, in all three of the preceding spaced verses, Paul is talking about the present time—that is, when he initially wrote the letter to the Romans.

The main point of these three chapters is that while much of Israel's history was marked by self-righteousness, unbelief, and rebellion, there has always been a remnant of true Israelite (i.e., Jewish) believers. Paul wants the Gentile Christians in Rome to understand that they should not become proud and think God's plan of salvation is now only for the Gentiles. Note the following clear references to Gentile pride in Romans chapter 11: "do not consider yourself to be superior to those other branches" (v. 18); "Do not be arrogant, but tremble" (v. 20); "so that you may not be conceited" (v. 25). These references (NIV) are very significant.

Throughout the three chapters, Paul focuses on the remnant believers of Israel, and he starts this focusing at the outset.

After listing the advantages of being an Israelite in 9:4–5, Paul immediately says, "For not all who are descended from Israel are Israel. Nor because they are his descendants are they all Abraham's children" (9:6–7). Of particular importance is Paul's dual usage of the word Israel in 9:6. This distinguishing of ethnic Israel from remnant Israel is continued later in 9:27–33 and 10:16, 21. It is also noteworthy that Paul made this distinction earlier in the letter: "A man is not a Jew if he is only one outwardly, nor is circumcision merely outward and physical. No a man is a Jew if he is one inwardly; and circumcision is circumcision of the heart, by the Spirit, not by the written code" (Rom. 2:28–29).

Now, let us analyze Romans chapter 11. After using himself as a present-day example of divine grace and election among ethnic Israel in verse 1, and then referring to a similar past example associated with the prophet Elijah in verses 2–4, Paul goes on to say, "So too, at the present time there is a remnant chosen by grace" (v. 5). Again, Paul is emphasizing (a) the present time, and (b) the believing remnant of ethnic Israel. So Paul is interchangeably talking about ethnic Israel in general (vv. 1a, 2a, 7a) and remnant Israel (vv. 4–5, 7b), which is crucial to understanding the chapter as a whole. The point is that the context of certain Pauline nouns and pronouns determines the intended meaning thereof.

Subsequently, he refers to two Old Testament scriptures in verses 8–10 to emphasize that there has always been a part of ethnic Israel that was/is spiritually hardened. Paul then talks about how ethnic Israel's present hardening or unbelief has resulted in ministry and blessing among the Gentiles, which in turn, can result in making (remnant) Israel envious and accepting of God's salvation (vv. 11–16). The contexts of verses 11ff indicate who (i.e., what specific Israel) Paul is referring to—either ethnic Israel in general or remnant Israel. The fact that Paul in verses 13f refers, first, to his ministry to the Gentiles and, second, to his hope that "some" ethnic Israel will be envious and thus saved, indicates that Paul in verses 11–15 is distinguishing between hardened ethnic Israel and envious remnant Israel. It is also obvious from verses 13f that Paul in verses 11–15 is referring to the time when he was living. Paul then discusses in verses 17–24 (a) how believing Gentiles are like a wild olive branch that is grafted into the natural olive tree, (b) that believing Gentiles must not become proud and think they are more deserving than unbelieving Israelites, for the former are "wild" while the latter are "natural," albeit cut off, and (c) how unbelieving Israelites (if they believe) can be regrafted back into their own olive tree. Again, Paul is referring to the present time, which is reflected in his statement about Israelites, "And if they do not persist in unbelief, they will be grafted in, for God is able to graft them in again" (v. 23).

The main point of Paul's argument regarding the grafting of Gentiles and the regrafting of Israelites is that they are related processes which pertain to the present time or age. Paul began this chapter by asking the question, "Did God reject his people?" (v. 1), and the apostle's answer up to verses 24 deals not with the nation of Israel in the distant future, but with the believing regrafted remnant of Israel in the present age. So chapters 9, 10, and the first twenty-four verses of chapter 11, all pertain to the present time. The big question now is, are those interpreters correct who say that the remaining verses, 25–32, refer to the eschatological future? In other words, does the statement by Paul in verse 26a, "And so all Israel will be saved" (KJV), which is also rendered "and in this way all Israel will be saved" (NIV), refer to a distant future experience of ethnic/national Israel, or does it refer to some kind of more immediate or present phenomenon?

As we analyze Romans 11:25–32, we must first remember that the theme of verses 11–24 is the regrafting of remnant ethnic Israel at the present time. It is imperative to note that Paul's reference to the pride of the Gentile Roman believers in verse 25b confirms (a) that his focus is still on the present time and (b) that remnant (regrafted) ethnic Israel is still in Paul's mind. Paul wants the Gentile Roman believers to understand "this mystery" (v. 25a), which implies he has already been referring to it, and it is this mystery that will impair pride from arising among the Gentile Roman believers. So the mystery is summed up in the words, "all Israel will be saved" (v. 26a). Thus this mystery has to do with the regrafting of remnant ethnic Israel due to the envying of Gentile believers.

This mystery is substantiated by the immediate preceding verses 22–24, and the subsequent verses 30–31, where in the latter, the mystery is explained again and the word "now" describes the mystery as a present phenomenon. Verses 26bc–29 must be interpreted within this contextual framework. Suffice it to say that a very strong contextual and grammatical case can be made that the latter "Israel" in verse 26 refers to the (past and present) remnant of ethnic Israel. For more substantiation of this grammatical (and contextual) case, I recommend chapter 6 of O. Palmer Robertson's book *The Israel of God*. There is also some merit to the case that "all Israel" in verse 26 refers to both (remnant) ethnic Israel and Gentile believers, as verse 25d refers to "the full number of the Gentiles has come in," which is followed by "and in this way all Israel will be saved."

More importantly, for the purposes of this essay, the contextual basis for the Christian Zionist claim that "all Israel" refers to ethnic/national Israel in the eschatological future is not only arbitrary and sorely weak, but it is completely deficient. I repeat, "all Israel" in Romans 11:26 either refers to the remnant believers of ethnic Israel, or to all Jewish and Gentile believers that comprise true Israel. But "all Israel" definitely does not refer to ethnic/national Israel in the distant end-times scenario. May I remind you that Paul earlier used the word Israel in Romans 9:6 to refer to a subset of ethnic/national Israel. The fact remains that nowhere in the book of Romans, including chapters 9–11, does Paul discuss or infer eschatological (i.e., future) events. When will evangelical and Pentecostal Christians admit their interpretation of Romans 11:25–26 has often been misconstrued, shoddy, and erroneous? I am flabbergasted that there have been so many otherwise good evangelical theologians who have essentially ignored the preceding contextual (and grammatical) criteria. The use of Romans 11:25–26 is a most flimsy theological foundation for the mistaken idea that is called Christian Zionism.

The term Israel is used seventy-one times in the New Testament—twelve times each in Matthew and Luke, twice in Mark, four times in John, eighteen times in Acts, seventeen times in Paul's letters, and three times each in Hebrews and Revelation. Usually the term Israel is descriptive and refers to the historic nation of Israel. Of the seventeen usages in Paul's letters, eleven usages are in Romans chapters 9–11, one of which does not depict ethnic/national Israel, that being Romans 9:6. So Paul used the term Israel six times in his other twelve letters, another one of which definitely does not refer to ethnic/national Israel, that being the "Israel of God" mentioned in Galatians 6:16.

The pertinent point is that nowhere in Jesus's teachings, Paul's letters, or the book of Revelation is there any clear reference to the restoration of ethnic/national Israel. The initial New Testament references or allusions to the restoration of Israel associated with such people as Simeon (Luke 2:25), Anna (Luke 2:38), and Jesus's disciples (Luke 24:21; Acts 1:6), show that the "restoration of Israel" was an old covenant term that was clarified and reworded with the expanded revelation of the new covenant. The New Testament overwhelmingly emphasizes the "kingdom of God" and its international composition.

There is nothing in the New Testament that says or infers the Jewish people or state deserve special treatment. Rather the New Testament says Christians should be prioritizing love, prayer, evangelism, discipleship, and the ministry of the Holy Spirit for all nations. In Matthew 5:48, Jesus Christ tells us to "be perfect, therefore, as your heavenly Father is perfect." The context of this verse has to do with unconditional and unbounded love for *all people.* In Mark 11:17, when Jesus cleared the temple, he emphasized, "My house will be called a house of prayer for *all nations.*" In Mark 16:15, Jesus Christ tells us to, "go into all the *world* and preach the good news to *all creation.*" In Matthew 28:19, Jesus Christ tells us, "Therefore go and make disciples of *all nations.*" In Acts 1:8, after he was resurrected, Jesus Christ told his disciples, "But you will receive power when the Holy Spirit comes on you;

and you will be my witnesses in Jerusalem, and in all Judea and Samaria, and *to the ends of the earth.*"

The thrust of the remaining New Testament, from the book of Romans to that of Revelation, has to do with the peoples/ nations of the world. The point is that Christian Zionists err grievously when they do not prioritize love, prayer, evangelism, discipleship, and the ministry of the Holy Spirit for all people. Where, pray tell, does it say in the New Testament that Christians should give political and military support to the people/state of Israel? Christian Zionists also err when their efforts to minister to the legitimate practical needs of the people of Israel are not matched by similar efforts to minister to the legitimate practical needs of adjacent non-Jewish peoples.

Conclusion

Each of the four main points of this essay presentation is devastating to Christian Zionism, and together, cumulatively, the four points totally shatter the theoretical/theological basis of the Christian Zionist project. Let me restate these four points.

Point #1. The Old Testament Abrahamic covenant cannot be isolated from the Mosaic covenant and other subsequent divine covenants. (Christian Zionism isolates the Abrahamic covenant.)

Point #2. The Old Testament prophetic "Restoration of Israel" has to do with an eschatological Messianic kingdom of belief. (Christian Zionism has to do with a temporal nation of unbelief.)

Point #3. The New Testament teaches that the Messiah (Jesus Christ) supremely fulfills the Israelite faith of the Old Testament. (Christian Zionism subtly downplays the role and ramifications of the Messiah.)

Point #4. The New Testament prioritizes Christian ministry (i.e., love, prayer, evangelism, discipleship, and the ministry of the Holy Spirit) for all nations. (Christian Zionism prioritizes practical, political, and military aid for one nation.)

If you are a Christian Zionist, what is the scriptural basis of your belief? I maintain your belief is due to (a) a misconstrued sentimentalism toward the Jewish people and (b) a shoddy exegesis (i.e., analysis) of scripture. This sentimentalism was evident in the work of several (Christian) pioneer Zionist politicians such as Lord Shaftesbury (1801–85), Arthur Balfour (1848–1930), and David Lloyd George (1863–1945). While these Englishmen undoubtedly had England's geopolitical interests in mind, they also sincerely thought they were helping solve the "Jewish problem" (i.e., what to do with the Jews). They wanted to help the Jews, for Jesus Christ was a Jew. The degree to which Christian Zionist sentiment contributed to the creation of modern Israel is an interesting historical and academic question but one that is beyond the scope of this essay.

What historical and contemporary Christian Zionists did not and do not totally understand is that the Jewish problem, and the specific relationship between Jewish people and their ancient homeland, is rooted in the divine covenant of the Bible. The land promise of the divine covenant associated with Abraham, Moses, and the Old Testament prophets was and is conditional on faith and obedience. What I am saying is that the reunification of the people and land of Israel in 1948 CE was humankind's arbitrary attempt, without faith and obedience, and without the Davidic Messiah, to undo what God sovereignly decreed two to four thousand years ago. The idea that the creation of Israel in 1948 CE was a direct fulfillment of prophecy and a harbinger of things to come is misled and artificial. Of course, this is a hard pill to swallow for a lot of evangelical and Pentecostal Christians, as they have had this idea foisted on them so strongly.

Shame on evangelical and Pentecostal teachers and leaders for allowing a psuedobiblical idea to mislead, confuse, and divide many of God's people. Shame on "theological dispensationalism," which is the root of this idea, and which deserves to be discredited. Foremost, the dispensationalist tenet that the word Israel in the Old and New Testaments always refers to the physical Jewish people/nation is clearly wrong. The related dispensationalist tenet that there are two distinct divine plans, one for Jews and one for Christians, is also clearly wrong. Suffice it to say that modern Zionism cannot be legitimized on the basis of Old and New Testament theology. If one endeavors to legitimize modern Zionism, they must base their position on historical, humanitarian, and democratic principles. Likewise, if Christians want to support modern Israel, they must do so on historical, humanitarian, and democratic grounds. It must be said clearly and loudly that Christians do not have a "biblical mandate" to support the modern state of Israel.

I could not care less if Christian Zionist sympathizers call me anti-Semitic, for I call them antibiblical. I am simply trying to "correctly handle the word of truth," as it says in 2 Timothy 2:15. And I readily and happily admit that I am commanded by God to love Jews as well as Gentiles, which I try to do. Nonetheless, the Christian Zionist project was one of the biggest mistakes evangelical and Pentecostal Christians made in the twentieth century, and this mistake not only offended a lot of people worldwide, but it also greatly impaired world evangelization. The Christian Zionist project showed unbiblical favoritism and failed to clearly communicate the good news of Jesus Christ to both Jews and Gentiles. The apostle Paul, if he was alive, would be furious. The Christian Zionist project was a classic case of zeal without knowledge. Admittedly, it was an "honest mistake," but then again zeal and sincerity have never demarked truth. And, yes, God has blessed and used the lives and ministries of many Christian Zionists, but he has graciously done so in spite of their error concerning Israel.

The bottom line of this essay presentation, whether you are a passionate or passive Christian Zionist, is this: Can you scripturally refute the four main points that were enunciated and explained? To admit you are or were wrong takes integrity and humility.

God Did Not Use Evolution

A Biblical Challenge to All Evangelical Theistic Evolutionists

DEFINITION: THEISTIC EVOLUTION—THE IDEA THAT GOD used extensive (macro) evolution in the creation of the universe and living things. The three main variant forms are:

1. Theistic evolution proper. Genesis tells us the "who" and "why" of creation, whereas naturalistic science tells us the "how" and "when." The Genesis creation account is figurative. God is sovereign over the naturalistic evolutionary process.

2. Progressive creation. There were long periods of naturalistic evolution interspersed with some divine fiat creations. The Genesis days of creation can be (a) literal and separated by geological epochs or (b) figurative and representative of geological epochs.

3. The gap theory. There was an original pre-Adamic creation (Gen. 1:1), which was followed by a tremendous time gap (i.e., the geological ages, hence the positing of evolutionary development). Genesis 1:2 ("Now the earth became formless and empty,") then describes the earth after a great cataclysm (i.e., the fall of Lucifer/Satan) had altered or ruined the earth's previous condition. Genesis 1:3ff thus describes the detailed seven-day history of re-creation.

The conviction that God has not used extensive (macro) evolution in his plan for this world has steadily remained in my mind and heart for many years. I also think there is an irrefutable biblical case for holding this conviction. Frankly, I am tired of reading articles and books written by evangelical Christians that promote, accommodate, or entertain theistic evolution, and the same can be said about Christian videos and online presentations. Furthermore, it disturbs me that many evangelical colleges, seminaries, and universities either nonchalantly promote theistic evolution or are open to variant forms of the same.

Before I go any further, it needs to be stated at the outset that I unapologetically adhere to the historical-grammatical method of interpreting the Bible. This simply means that one strives to understand the words and sentences (and figures of speech) in the customary, historical sense, as the authors intended. Apart from this basic hermeneutical method, biblical interpretation becomes unduly subjective and capricious. Thus Edward J. Young's following comment is pertinent: "It is of course true that the Bible is not a textbook of science, but all too often, it would seem, this fact is made a pretext for treating lightly the content of Genesis one. Inasmuch as the Bible is the Word of God, whenever it speaks on any subject, whatever that subject may be, it is accurate in what it says."

In this essay, I will be presenting a biblical case for fiat special creation—"fiat" meaning immediate creation(s) by the sheer will and word of God Almighty, including the concept of creation ex nihilo (out of nothing), this concept being inferred in Genesis 1:1, and affirmed in Hebrews 11:3; "special" referring to the distinct nature of God's creative activity, as revealed in Genesis chapters 1–2, contrary to evolution's homologous gradualism. The reason for including the adjective "special" is to leave no doubt about the intended meaning, as the term "fiat creation" is sometimes used by theistic evolutionists. I might add that proponents of theistic evolution often prefer the term "evolutionary creation," but I prefer the former term. Also, if you will note, there is hardly any reference to the question of time (i.e., when specifically God created everything), and this omission is done purposefully. Granted, the historical-grammatical hermeneutical method intimates a "young earth" creation. Nevertheless, it is paramount and sufficient to simply recognize God's immediate creations by means of his sheer will and word, and to recognize the distinct and consecutive nature of God's original creative activity.

Having said all this, I would like to issue, in a spirit of integrity and good will, a challenge to all evangelical theistic evolutionists. Rather than challenging them on scientific grounds, the crux of the issue has to do with the biblical record. Therefore, I challenge any and all evangelical theistic evolutionists to address and biblically refute the following five points.

Point #1: The primary means or repository of divine revelation is the inspired, written Word of God (i.e., the Bible), not nature (i.e., creation).

Of course, most evangelical Christians would say they adhere to this first point, "repository" meaning a place where something is stored. God's character, plan, and will are revealed, most specifically, through special revelation (i.e., the inspired scriptures). While the Old Testament book of Genesis includes the earliest records of divine and human activity relative to this physical realm, and while the historical composition and compilation of this book are somewhat obscure, the fact remains that the complete book of Genesis has always been viewed, by both Jews and Christians, as being part of the inspired scriptures. The book of Genesis has also historically been associated with Moses, who talked to God "face to face" (Exod. 33:11), the implication being the Genesis creation account was endorsed, by both Moses and God, to be trustworthy and true. The Protestant Reformation slogan "sola scriptura" (by scripture only) was formulated to champion the primacy of scripture, this tenet being derived from such biblical references as Matthew 4:4; Luke 24:44f; 2 Peter 1:20f; and 2 Timothy 3:16. At the same time, scriptures such as Psalm 19:1–4; Romans 1:18–21, and

Romans 2:14–16, indicate that God has also revealed himself somewhat through general revelation (i.e., nature).

But apart from these scriptures in Psalm 19, and Romans chapters 1–2, there is hardly any other enunciated emphasis, in the whole Bible, on the idea or doctrine of general revelation. Consequently, the idea that God's world is on the same revelatory par as God's Word is totally foreign to the Old and New Testaments, and this is the essence of this point #1. Also, Christians have historically believed, and rightly so, that the special and general modes of revelation would not contradict each other, as God is not a deceiver.

Regarding the creation of the universe and living things, there should be no question as to which mode of revelation (i.e., the inspired scriptures or nature) is more authoritative for evangelical Christians. But there is a lingering question on this topic among a sizable number of evangelical Christians, who say they believe in the authority/primacy of scripture, but then do not actually exhibit such a belief. Thus their viewpoints and writings are either overtly or covertly based on the primacy of nature (i.e., naturalistic criteria), plus the fact that they invariably ignore most or all of the remaining scriptural points of this essay. These theistic evolutionists ought to fess up and admit they are inexorably driven by a latent precommitment to philosophical naturalism (i.e., the idea that natural law is supreme). For example, I just finished reading an expressly self-described and peer-endorsed "evangelical" recent book that discusses naturalistic criteria first, then biblical criteria—the latter in which the author denies the historicity of Genesis chapters 1–11.

In conclusion to point 1, a belief in the primacy of scripture is one of the main defining features of what it means to be an evangelical Christian. It is misleading for evangelical theistic evolutionists to say they adhere to the primacy of scripture, when in fact, they do not. It is questionable indeed whether these theistic evolutionists even have the right to call themselves "evangelical." If one is an evangelical theistic evolutionist, the onus is on them to substantiate their case from the scriptures (and refute the scriptural case for fiat special creation). Therefore, this point can be recast in the following question: What are you going to trust—the surety of the revealed, inscripturated Word of God, or the vagaries of a priori naturalistic evolutionism? Consequently, by being based on philosophical dogma (i.e., naturalistic evolutionism), rather than biblical criteria, theistic evolution diminishes the Bible's authority as the primary means or repository of divine revelation.

Point #2: A historical-grammatical study of the Old Testament words *yom* (day) and *yamim* (days) supports fiat special creation, not evolutionary creation in any sense.

Although the Hebrew word yom can sometimes refer to a period of time, as it does in Genesis 1:5, 14, 16, 18 (depicting daylight), and Genesis 2:24 (depicting the entire creation week), the same word cannot legitimately be interpreted as such when it is used to describe the respective six/seven days of creation (Gen. 1:5–6, 8, 13, 19, 23, 31; 2:2f). First, the normal definition of the word yom in the Hebrew Bible is a day of the week. Context invariably elucidates this normal, or any alternative, meaning.

Second, whenever the word yom is accompanied by a number (e.g., second day), the meaning is always a literal day, and there are over one hundred cases of this usage in the first five books of the Old Testament, including the creation day references in Genesis chapter 1. Furthermore, in the Old Testament as a whole, the word yom is accompanied by a numerical adjective about 350 times, and in virtually every case, it denotes a literal day.

Third, the phrase "evening and morning," which is repeatedly used immediately prior to the numerical adjective in Genesis chapter 1, is a Hebrew term that is associated with a literal day. There are twenty cases in the first five books of the Old Testament where the Hebrew words for "evening" and "morning" are used together, and in every case, the meaning is one of literal days. This pattern of literal days is continued in the thirteen remaining Old Testament cases where these two words are used together (with the exception of apocalyptic Daniel 8:14, 26). Fourth, the creation week—Jewish week parallel in Exodus 20:8–11 and 31:17, which significantly was prescribed verbatim by God, further supports the orthodox literal interpretation, the implication being that the literal seven-day Jewish week followed the literal pattern set forth by God in the creation week. Additionally, the Hebrew plural word yamim (days) is used over seven hundred times in the Old Testament, and in every case, it refers to literal days. Thus in Exodus 20:11, where the LORD says that "in six days the LORD made the heavens and the earth, the sea, and all that is in them," there can be no doubt that six literal days were intended. Exodus 31:17 confirms the same literal intention.

It is also very significant that "the heavens and the earth" in Exodus 20:11 and 31:17 are the exact Hebrew words used in Genesis 1:1. So not only does a historical-grammatical study of the word yamim (days) support fiat special creation, but God's words recorded in Exodus 20:11 and 31:17 indicate that Genesis 1:1 is directly associated with the six days of creation as revealed in the subsequent verses of Genesis chapter 1.

Yet some evangelical scholars balk on the literal interpretation and suggest that yom may have been the best or only word available to use. Victor P. Hamilton (*New International Commentary*) entertains this so-called literary interpretation whereby "God reveals himself to his people in a medium with which they can identify and which they can comprehend." But the problem with this view is that it still ignores all the pertinent aforementioned historical-grammatical criteria.

These literary interpreters are thus guilty of arbitrarily downplaying the meaning of the text. Even if one concedes, as I do, that the divine creation days of Genesis chapter 1 may not have been precise twenty-four-hour days, the fact remains the words and tenor of Genesis chapter 1, and later related references in the Pentateuch, simply do not intimate, in any way, the days of creation to be long periods of time, and this fact is the essence of this main point #2. All the information that God has given us in his inspired written Word indicates his original creation was (a) by fiat (e.g., the creation of light in Gen. 1:3), (b) special (i.e., involving distinct acts), and (c) consecutive (i.e., chronological). For example, the numbering of the "days," and the "evening and morning" references indicate separate and spaced creation acts. Furthermore, surely God could and would have communicated to us more accurately if the creation week was, in fact, spread out over millions of years. If the million-year scenario were true, God would be misleading at best, and a liar at worst. And it also would seem very strange if God initiated and sustained his creation for millions, even billions, of years prior to his main creative purpose—that purpose being the creation of humankind.

A brief explanation is also necessary regarding a primary scripture that supposedly supports the metaphoric usage, that scripture(s) being 2 Peter 3:8 (Ps. 90:4)—"With the Lord a day is like a thousand years, and a thousand years are like a day." Foremost, it is noteworthy indeed that this passage differentiates a day from a thousand years. The underlying contextual meaning of the passage is that God transcends, or stands outside of, time. Using 2 Peter 3:8 to posit a lengthy creation schedule is clearly a case of reading something into the text that is not there.

With respect to the first four days of creation, when the sun, moon, and stars were not yet created, the consistent literal interpretation is not in jeopardy when one recognizes that God is eternal, sovereign, and omnipotent. Thus God is not limited by space-time constraints. In other words, God could have instituted linear time (i.e., the space-time universe) when he initially created the "heavens" and the "earth" in Genesis 1:1, and in turn ordain the first four days of creation to be literal (twenty-four-hour) days as we know them (without the subsequently designated roles of the sun, moon, and stars in determining time—Genesis 1:14), and his

Word seems to say that he did just that. Interestingly, Genesis chapter 1 simply states that God caused light to shine from a source other than the sun for the first three days, which is reminiscent of Revelation 22:5 where a re-created world is filled with light without the sun.

The reason I have allowed for a quasi-literal interpretation of day/days is simply because the sun, moon, and stars were not created until day four. On the other hand, the first day of creation included the differentiation of darkness and light and was followed by the phrases "And there was evening, and there was morning," these criteria connoting the concept of a literal day.

In conclusion to point 2, the historical-grammatical burden of proof lies totally with those who adopt a metaphoric interpretation of the Hebrew words yom and yamim. The preceding cumulative (biblical) argument firmly establishes a literal historical-grammatical meaning for the specified usage of yom in Genesis. Perhaps most importantly, the fact undeniably remains that Moses and his Hebrew successors interpreted the Genesis creation account to be one of fiat special creation (although they did not call it that) in six or seven consecutive literal days. Consequently, when people skeptically ask me if I honestly believe God created everything in six literal days (and a literal seventh day of rest which is inferred), I answer by saying they were either six literal days or six quasi-literal days, but they were nothing that was compatible with evolutionary theory. I might add that it is arrogant for puny human beings, who really have no idea of creation's profundity, to question that which God has chosen to reveal in his Word about the matter.

The knowledge gap about creation that exists, due to God's nondisclosure and humanity's sin-tainted finiteness, needs to be bridged by faith—a faith in the trustworthiness of God and his written Word. Just as we human beings do not understand how God created ex nihilo (out of nothing), similarly, we do not understand how God created everything in six/seven literal or quasi-literal days. As well as faith in God, the doctrine of fiat special creation requires a goodly dose of humility before God. This should not surprise us, as humility is the crown virtue of the godly life.

Lastly, it is important to note that, by arbitrarily discounting the historical-grammatical hermeneutical meaning of the Hebrew words yom and yamim, theistic evolution casts doubt upon the reliability of Genesis and the scriptures as a whole. The (so-called evangelical) alternatives to a literal or quasi-literal creation week actually render the early chapters of Genesis to be unintelligible. What I am saying is that we evangelicals need to be consistent in applying the historical-grammatical hermeneutical method of interpreting scripture.

Point #3: The book of Genesis depicts historical continuity, not nonhistorical prose or mythology.

Theistic evolution proper, as I have called it, says that Genesis chapters 1–3 is some kind of nonhistorical literary or mythological device. This idea goes contrary to the following biblical factors.

To begin with, the intermittent, successive use of the Hebrew term, translated "these are the generations of" (King James Version), or "this is the account of" (New International Version), suggests factual history. There are eleven instances throughout the Genesis text where this extant genealogical term is used (i.e., Gen. 2:4; 5:1; 6:9; 10:1; 11:10, 27; 25:12,:19; 36:1, 9; 37:2). Interestingly enough, the first such reference to this consistently used term is as early as Genesis 2:4. Notwithstanding the scholarly debates regarding (a) whether this term is used in Genesis 2:4 to introduce or conclude a section and (b) whether this term reveals underlying written source material (i.e., colophons from cuneiform tablets), the historical nature of "later" content in Genesis (as demarcated by Gen. 25:12, 19; 36:1, 9; 37:2) most definitely weighs in favor of the historical nature of "early" content in Genesis (as demarcated by Gen. 2:4; 5:1; 6:9; 10:1; 11:10, 27). The point or strong inference is that all of Genesis, including chapters 1–3, is written as a historical narrative.

Another significant factor, which has already been discussed somewhat under point #1, is the use of the phrase "the heavens and the earth" in Genesis 2:4, this verse most likely being a heading that introduces the succeeding section, and thus the succeeding section is associated with the preceding section, as the same phrase (i.e., "the heavens and the earth") is used earlier in Genesis 2:1 and 1:1. We must also recognize the significance of the geohistorical allusions in Genesis chapter 2 (i.e., Eden, Pishon, Havilah, Gihon, Cush, Tigris, Asshur, and Euphrates—Gen. 2:10–14). These allusions testify to the geohistoricity of Genesis chapter 2 (including the Garden of Eden, which also implies the tree with the forbidden fruit, the serpent, the individual man, the individual woman, et cetera). Thus these explicit and implicit geohistorical allusions in Genesis chapter 2 also lend testimony to the geohistoricity of the complete Genesis text. Keep in mind that the consensus of many, if not most, historical and contemporary evangelical Christian scholars is that Genesis chapters 1–2 are not separate creation accounts but are rather related, with the second chapter both complementing the first chapter and amplifying the sixth day of creation. After all, Jesus himself combined Genesis 1:27 and Genesis 2:24, as recorded in Matthew 19:4f and Mark 10:6–8.

Consider the Hebrew word *adam*, which can be (a) a generic term meaning "man" or "mankind," (b) a noun with an article meaning something like "the man," or (c) a proper name "Adam." Although the usage of the word adam in Genesis 1:26–27 and 5:1b, 2 are generic in nature, and 2:5 and 4:1b refer to other male persons, the remaining twenty-eight usages in Genesis chapters 1–5 refer to the same historical person. In other words, twenty-eight of the thirty-four times adam is used in Genesis chapters 1–5, it refers to the same individual, historical person. In Genesis chapter 2, this man was put in a garden with a woman made from his side (i.e., the very first woman). In chapter 3, the man and the woman disobeyed God and were put out of the garden. In chapter 4, the man and the woman started a family with three sons— Cain, Abel, and Seth, the oldest son's history recorded with several details. In chapter 5, the man's genealogical lineage, through his third son, is recorded to the tenth generation. The text also says in Genesis 3:20: "The man named his wife Eve, because she would become the mother of all the living." Thus Genesis 3:20 links Eve with Genesis 1:26–27, where it mentions "male and female he created them," and "Be fruitful and increase in number." Eve's association and complementary relationship with Adam indicates she was an individual, historical person.

Furthermore, the genealogical (Adam to Noah) list in Genesis chapter 5, which is identically copied in 1 Chronicles chapter 1 and Luke chapter 3, indicates historical validity and continuity, plus the fact that Adam is portrayed in these three lists as an individual person. The point is that Genesis chapters 2–4 (and chap. 5) is a historical narrative, rather than some kind of literary or mythological prose.

Then there is the New Testament, where throughout, Adam is also considered the first historical human being, rather than some kind of hominid or archetype that theistic evolutionists sometimes erroneously propose. The following New Testament scriptures support a historical Adam: Luke 3:37; Acts 17:26; Romans 5:12–19; 1 Corinthians 15:21f, 45–49; 1 Timothy 2:13f; Jude 14. Referring to Adam and Jesus Christ, Romans 5:18f reads, "Consequently, just as one trespass resulted in condemnation for all people, so also one righteous act resulted in justification and life for all people. For just as through the disobedience of the one man the many were made sinners, so also through the obedience of the one man the many will be made righteous." 1 Corinthians 15:21f reads, "For since death came through a man, the resurrection of the dead comes also through a man. For as in Adam all die, so in Christ all will be made alive." So, if we are not sure about the historicity and truth of the "first Adam," and thus what we call original sin, does this not undermine the need for and truth of the "last Adam" (Jesus Christ—1 Cor. 15:45), and his redeeming work on the cross?

Granted, the first Adam, after Genesis chapter 5, is essentially absent from the remaining Old Testament text, but the crucial concept of animal blood sacrifice (for sins) is seemingly initiated immediately after his (Adam's) sin (Gen. 3:21), and successively continued thereafter by Abel (Gen. 4:4), Noah (Gen. 8:20f), Abram (Gen. 12:8), the patriarchs, Moses and the Israelites, and the Levitical priesthood in general, until the ultimate blood sacrifice by the Lord Jesus Christ. In other words, Adam's sin had far-reaching subsequent historical consequences in terms of blood sacrifice. It should also be noted that in Luke 11:51, Jesus refers to and verifies the historical death of Adam and Eve's son Abel, plus the fact there are a few other references in the New Testament to Cain and Abel (e.g., Heb. 11:4; 1 John 3:12). Additionally, the apostle Paul, in 2 Corinthians 11:3 and 1 Timothy 2:13f, confirmed that Eve was an individual, historical person.

May I simply say that all the contemporary discourse and skepticism in evangelical circles concerning the historical Adam reminds me of the ill-conceived and doomed scholarly "quest for the historical Jesus" of the nineteenth and twentieth centuries. Just as some former scholars tried to dissect and disprove the New Testament gospel account/portrait of Jesus of Nazareth, some present-day "evangelical" scholars are trying to dissect and disprove the Old Testament Genesis account/portrait of Adam and Eve. Suffice it to say both of these attempts have been based on arbitrary and antagonistic antisupernatural presuppositions.

A few words about the accommodation theory are also necessary. To say that later biblical characters and writers (and thus God, for he guided and inspired them) accommodated themselves to the cultural, literary, or mythological views of their Genesis ancestors is to arbitrarily deny the integrity of all parties involved. The accommodation theory also implies that we can never be certain whether any biblical statement is literary/mythological or historical. The fact of the matter is the Jews believed their religion was one of divine historical intervention, revelation, and inspiration, and not a religion influenced by Near Eastern creation myths with all their gods, goddesses, conflicts, killings, monsters, et cetera. Liberal (accommodation oriented) "evangelical" critics arbitrarily downplay this historical and revelatory essence of Old Testament religion, and while there may be some cultural connections in the earliest chapters of Genesis, these critics overplay the Near Eastern contextual component. Thus the liberal theological insistence that parts of the Bible (especially the earliest chapters of Genesis) must be (re)interpreted in its Near Eastern "literary" or "mythological" context, is based on unfounded, forced, and often fanciful assumptions.

These critics say their goal is to understand the text the way the author wanted to be understood, without trying to read anything into it or squeeze anything out of it, and yet they are the ones reading things into the text and squeezing things out of the text. For example, when a critic says Adam is a literary "archetype" who embodies or represents all human beings, the question remains, Is this what the author wanted to be understood? So, according to these critics, the tree of life and all other details in Genesis chapters 2–3 are not truly historical. This line of thought is totally unacceptable.

Two further allegations must be addressed, both of which are used by some evangelicals to justify a nonhistorical interpretation of the Genesis creation account. First, it is alleged that the sole purpose of the Genesis creation account was the affirmation of monotheism (i.e., the exclusive one-God concept) in the midst of a pervasively polytheistic and idolatrous ancient Near Eastern world. In other words, rather than a historical depiction, it is deemed that the overriding purpose of the Genesis creation account was to simply declare that the earth, sun, moon, stars, animals, man, et cetera, were all created by God, thus denigrating the deification and worship of these things.

The second allegation has to do with days one through three in Genesis (pertaining to light, sky, water, and land) being parallel to days four through six (pertaining to light bearers, sky and water dwellers, and land dwellers), the implication being that these parallels indicate the account is symmetrical and figurative, rather than sequential and historical. Although both of these allegations initially appear reasonable, I believe they are misled. Genesis chapter 1 most definitely affirms monotheism, and there may be a pattern to the schedule of divine creation acts, but to insist that these peculiarities reveal the raison d'etre of the chapter is arbitrary.

Furthermore, we must always keep in mind that the historical-grammatical hermeneutical burden of proof lies with those who maintain the Genesis creation account was something other than a factual, historical depiction. The truth of the matter (no pun intended) is that theistic evolutionists do not want to admit the earth was initially created on days one through three prior to the creation of the sun and stars on day four, for this biblical scenario contradicts evolutionary theory, which states the stars and sun were created before the earth. Oh, the wisdom and majesty of God's creative ways as recorded in Genesis chapter 1, which clearly states the earth is the focal point of this physical universe.

Let us now consider the important matter of interpreting the very first two verses of Genesis: "In the beginning God created the heavens and the earth (v. 1). Now the earth was formless and empty, darkness was over the surface of the deep, and the Spirit of God was hovering over the waters" (v. 2 New International Version). To begin with, the fact remains that the "earth" is referred to in each of these verses.

Additionally, a face value reading of Genesis 1:1–2 indicates the "heavens" and the "waters" were also part of God's initial creation prior to the creation of "light" in Genesis 1:3–5. That Genesis 1:1–2 refers to some initial creative activity is especially attested to by the subsequent reference to "waters" in the verses describing the second day of creation (i.e., Gen. 1:6–7): "And God said, 'Let there be an expanse between the waters to separate water from water' (v. 6). So God made the expanse and separated the water under the expanse from the water above it. And it was so" (v. 7). In other words, the clear reference to "waters" in Genesis 1:6 presupposes and substantiates the authenticity and truth of the "waters" mentioned earlier in Genesis 1:2. And if the "waters" of Genesis 1:2 are authentic and true, that means the "earth" of Genesis 1:2 is also authentic and true. Keep in mind that the "waters" and "earth" of Genesis 1:2 are nowhere stated to be created after Genesis 1:1. Thus Genesis 1:1 must refer to some initial creative activity, for how else can one explain the existent "earth" and "waters" of Genesis 1:2?

Also, the creation of the earth prior to Genesis 1:3 correlates very well with what Genesis 1:9–10 actually says about the third creative day: "And God said, 'Let the water under the sky be gathered to one place, and let dry ground appear.' And it was so (v. 9). God called the dry ground 'land,' and the gathered waters he called 'seas'" (v. 10)." Thus the theme of separation in Genesis 1:4–10 is consistent with this historical interpretation. With the preceding rationale in mind, it is somewhat puzzling why many evangelical scholars persist in thinking that Genesis 1:1 is a mere summary statement introducing the six days of creative activity. In conclusion to what may appear to be a digression, the creation of the "waters" and the "earth" before Genesis 1:3 lends internal testimony to the historical authenticity and truth of the Genesis creation account, as Genesis 1:6–7 verifies Genesis 1:2 and 1:1.

This argument and conclusion also testifies against all figurative theories regarding the Genesis creation account. I also still maintain the historical nature of Genesis 1:1–2 is attested to by the use of the connecting word translated "and" or "now" (same Hebrew word) at the beginning of Genesis 1:2 and 1:3. Undoubtedly, the Bible explicitly and implicitly reveals more about creation than the bare fact that the biblical God is the creator. Are people like myself reading into the text when we say Genesis 1:1–5 records the material creation of the universe, earth, waters, darkness, and light on day one? Am I an extreme material reductionist when I am simply satisfied with a face value reading of Genesis chapter 1? I do not think so.

In summary, I think I have several excellent reasons for believing the book of Genesis depicts historical continuity. Most importantly, the crux of this third point has to do with where you draw the line between historical and nonhistorical events in the book of Genesis, and on what basis that line is drawn. Apart from a completely historical interpretation, there is simply no legitimate basis to draw any such line.

Point #4. The book of Genesis, and the Bible as a whole, describes a finished, stable, and tainted creation, not a continuous, dynamic, and progressive (evolutionary) creation.

Theistic evolutionists are hard-pressed to refute this point (as they are with all five of these points). I remember talking to a Bible college teacher many years ago who said this point alone kept him from entertaining any theistic evolutionary ideas. The Bible simply does not support the concept of a continuous, dynamic, and progressive (evolutionary) creation. Furthermore, those Christians who adhere to a theory whereby God used evolution in the past but does so no longer, have the added burden of justifying this inconsistency on the part of the creator. These Christians are also in the contradictory position of denying the corpus of evolutionary theory, that corpus being the so-called scientific evidence that purportedly indicates that evolution is a present, as well as a past, phenomenon. Therefore, a critique of theistic evolution most definitely includes a critique of its continuous, dynamic, and progressive traits.

The "continuous" trait highlights the ongoing scope of evolution over eons of time (including the past, present, and future). Contrarily, the Bible clearly states that God rested after the six creation days, for his creation was finished

(Gen. 2:1–3). There is no intimation whatsoever, in the Bible, that the creation of this temporal world is continuous, unfinished, and in the process of becoming. The "dynamic" trait refers to the inherent power within and changeability of all creation, as all creation, it is deemed, is given to evolution. Contrarily, there is no positive biblical basis for this trait either, plus the fact that the Genesis descriptive phrase "according to their kinds" (Gen. 1:11–12, 21, 24, 25) implies a certain measure of genetic stability for all living things. Likewise, the Judeo-Christian concept whereby God sustains the world (Job 38:1ff; Col. 1:17; Heb. 1:3) implies a modicum of temporal stability. This concept focuses on the creator's sovereign, sustaining power, rather than any quasi-miraculous power inherent in creation that essentially causes macroevolutionary metamorphosis. The "progressive" trait claims the continuous, dynamic evolutionary process is one of intrinsic improvement (i.e., creation is getting better). Contrarily, the Bible says that creation was "good" (Gen. 1:10, 12, 18, 21, 25), even "very good" (Gen. 1:31), at the beginning of history.

The Bible also indicates that the fall of Adam and Eve was a negative step that incurred retrogressive (tainted) consequences for humankind and the world at large. Not only were Adam and Eve and their descendants estranged from the presence and perfectibility of God (Gen. 3:21–24; Rom. 5:12, 18–19), but God also cursed the earth (Gen.

3:17–19; Romans 8:20–22). In other words, Adam and Eve fell downward, not upward. Furthermore, there is absolutely nothing in what the Bible says about eschatology (i.e., end-time events) that indicates the universe and humankind will have progressively evolved prior to the Second Coming of Jesus Christ.

The fact that human beings are separated from God and are desperately in need of a Savior to reconcile them back to God, plus the fact that creation needs God's overt intervention to be restored to a state of paradise (Acts 3:21), both go contrary to the possibilities or inferences of progressive theistic evolutionary theory. For inherent in theistic evolutionary theory is the (tempting) possibility or inference that, since the universe and humankind have undergone, and are undergoing subtle evolution, all the problems in the universe, and within humankind, may eventually be rectified by this subtle principle alone, rather than by God's overt intervention or agency. Thus a case can be made that the progressive trait of theistic evolutionary theory is a contributing factor to the downplaying of overt divine agency in much contemporary Christian theology and experience. After all, if divine agency is more subtle than we have thought regarding creation, the question arises as to where else divine agency is more subtle than we have thought. Granted, God's providential agency is subtle at times, but the Bible clearly refers to God's overt, dynamic, miraculous agency as well. By now, it should be getting clearer how the continuous, dynamic, and progressive theory of evolutionary creation (i.e., theistic evolution) is not only contrary to the Bible, but also downplays, if not negates, the concept of "divine miracle."

Point #5: The Noahic flood was global, not regional (thus the full geological implications of this massive catastrophic event must be appreciated, not depreciated).

Theistic evolutionists do not appreciate the fact, and full geological implications, of the Noahic flood recorded in Genesis chapters 6–9. Following are several reasons indicating that this flood was, most definitely, global, as opposed to regional.

1. **The source of the flood:** Genesis 7:11f says that "all the springs of the great deep burst forth, and the floodgates of the heavens were opened. And rain fell on the earth forty days and forty nights." The terms used here connote an unusual event, to say the least. Whereas it may not have rained prior to the flood (Gen. 2:5f, 9:11–17), torrents of water gushed from both underneath and overtop the earth. Undoubtedly, the two sources of water refer to the waters "under" and "above" of Genesis 1:6f.

2. **The duration of the flood:** A careful study of the Genesis text reveals that the flood spanned 371 days. The flood started in the six hundredth year of Noah's life, on the seventeenth day of the second month (Gen. 7:11). The ark rested on the mountains of Ararat on the seventeenth day of the seventh

month of Noah's six hundredth year, 150 days after the flood started (Gen. 8:3f). Consequently, the flood receded for more than 221 days before Noah came out of the ark in the six hundred and first year of his life, on the twenty-seventh day of the second month (Gen. 8:14). The computations from the relevant chapters in Genesis reveal a month was thirty days. Thus Noah and company were in the ark for over one whole year.

3. The depth of the flood: The floodwaters "rose greatly on the earth, and all the high mountains under the entire heavens were covered. The waters rose and covered the mountains to a depth of more than twenty feet" (Gen. 7:19f). In other words, the draft of the ark (i.e., the part in the water) was about twenty feet in depth. Furthermore, the fact that the ark finally rested on the "mountains of Ararat" (Gen. 8:4), which are fairly high (up to seventeen thousand feet), also supports the global argument.

4. The total destructiveness of the flood: The flood was God's judgment of the violence on the *earth*. Note that in Genesis 6:5–13, the Hebrew word for earth is mentioned eight times. The flood destroyed *all* people except Noah and company (Gen. 6:12f), and *all* life except marine life and life inside the ark (Gen. 6:7, 17; 7:23). In response to those who say these universal terms (e.g., earth, all) ought not to be interpreted literally, it must be noted that absolutely nothing in the text or context intimates such a figurative idiom, on the contrary. Additionally, Noah and family alone were righteous (Gen. 7:1), and the postflood earth was to be filled with Noah's descendants alone (Gen. 9:18f). Furthermore, God's covenant with Noah after the flood (Gen. chap. 9) seems meaningless if the flood was merely regional. Then there is the implication that God would be a liar, for he said he would never send such a flood again (Gen. 8:21; 9:11, 15), and millions have since perished in vast and destructive regional floods on the earth.

5. The size and need of the ark: On the basis that an ancient cubit was 17.5 inches, the ark was 437.5 feet long, 72.9 feet wide, and 43.7 feet high (Gen. 6:15). It had three decks (Gen. 6:16) and thus about 95,700 square feet of deck space. Why build a vessel of such size (the equivalent of 522 standard railway cars), if the flood was merely regional? It is more logical to think that the ark was built big to accommodate a great quantity of animal life, not to mention the fact that such a big boat would be able to withstand a huge, turbulent, catastrophic flood.

6. The supernatural element: The implied supernatural characteristic of the flood gives the global rendering credibility. For example, in Genesis 6:20, it says, "Two of every kind of bird, of every kind of animal and every kind of creature that moves along the ground will come to you to be kept alive." The supernatural element is also implied in Genesis 7:16 where it says that after Noah was safe in the ark with his family and the specified living creatures, "Then the LORD shut him in." If God brought the animals to the ark, and if God shut the door to enclose the animals inside the ark, it is also quite conceivable that God took care of the animals in the ark, and that he alleviated other practical and physical problems associated with the flood. Regional flood proponents are invariably guided by antisupernatural presuppositions, whereas the Bible is undeniably saturated with fantastic divine supernatural occurrences. When one reflects upon such biblical examples as the plagues in Egypt (Exod. chap. 7–12), and the parting of the Red Sea (Exod. chapter 14), not to mention other biblical miracles, the global extent of the Noahic flood is quite conceivable and feasible.

7. The biblical historicity of Noah: There are several additional biblical references (other than Gen. chap. 5–10) that substantiate the historicity of Noah and the flood (1 Chron. 1:4ff; Isa. 54:9; Ezek. 14:14, 20; Matt. 24:36–39; Luke 17:26–30; Heb. 11:7; 1 Pet. 3:20; 2 Pet. 2:5, 3:6). Note the affirmation by the Lord Jesus Christ. There is absolutely nothing in any of these references that suggests the flood was regional, on the contrary.

8. The Noahic flood—Second Coming analogy: Jesus Christ, and the apostle Peter, likened the Second Coming (of Jesus Christ) to the Noahic flood. Thus both the Second Coming and the Noahic flood are similarly depicted as sobering and global historical judgments (Luke 17:26–30; Matt. 24:36–39; 2 Pet. 3:3–7).

It is disturbing that this section regarding the Genesis flood needs to be written. For it is bewildering how some Christians (and Jews) can maintain the Genesis flood was regional. The burden of proof definitely lies with those who adopt such a view. And yet regional flood proponents rarely even mention the preceding discrepancies, let alone deal with them adequately. The cumulative biblical data (subpoints 1 to 8) indicates unequivocally that the flood was global. Frankly, the regional flood theory goes completely against everything recorded in scripture.

This tenet of a global flood is thus nonnegotiable for the devout Christian. Thus the geological implications of such a massive, catastrophic flood warrant painstaking attention and must not be neglected in the formulation of all earnest "creation—early earth" views espoused by Christians. Not only is "flood geology" a reasonable inference of a global flood, but it is an extremely probable inference at that. So the so-called geological column is most likely a result of this flood, and not a result of the presumable geological ages of presuppositional evolutionism. A lot could be said about the ever-increasing empirical data that supports the existence of a past, universal, primarily hydraulic, cataclysm (in other words, a past global flood), but that is not what this essay is all about.

Unfortunately, a large number of evangelical Christians are irrationally ignoring the pertinent biblical data regarding the Genesis flood event. The ranks of these irrational Christians include scientists, professionals, tradespeople, homemakers, businesspeople, students, Bible college professors, pastors, et cetera. These people, whether they realize it or not, are rebelling against God's Word. Needless to say, I find it most illuminating that virtually all professing evangelical scholars who adhere to variants of theistic evolution also maintain that the Genesis flood was not global. This fact in itself should cause us to be highly critical of theistic evolutionary theories. Since theistic evolution is covertly based on philosophical naturalism (i.e., geological uniformitarianism), its proponents instinctively and desperately know they cannot forfeit the (eonic) geological age factor. They cling to this factor in spite of the overwhelming biblical criteria against it.

In summary, God wants his people to adhere to his written Word and to rationality (not humanistic rationalism), and to "contend for the faith that was once for all entrusted to the saints" (Jude 3). The global extent of the Genesis flood is a tacit tenet of this revealed and entrusted Christian faith.

When the apparent problems of a global flood cause you to deny the Genesis record, you are allowing humanistic rationalism to sit in judgment upon the inscripturated Word of God. Consequently, if I ever came to believe the Genesis flood was regional (and not global), my belief in the Bible as God's Word would be shattered. Admittedly, I would be in a dire spiritual condition indeed. Now some people reading this will think such a reaction to be overly extreme, but I beg to differ with them, for I am only being rationally consistent. We are not discussing some minor textual variant here but rather a well-described formative event in what is believed to be the inspired written Word of God. If the Genesis flood account is suspect, so is everything else in the book of Genesis and the Bible as a whole. It is as simple as that.

Noah was called to trust God alone in the midst of an unbelieving and mocking world. He steadfastly believed the flood would come as God said, and it did come. We Christians are also in the midst of an unbelieving and mocking world. And we are similarly called to steadfastly believe and bear testimony to the same flood event, albeit in retrospect. As a matter of fact, both the apostle Peter (2 Pet. 3), and the Lord Jesus himself (Matt. 24:36ff), referred to the Genesis flood as the basis of their testimony concerning the judgment of the Second Coming (of Jesus Christ). Likewise, our testimony of this end-time global judgment (i.e., the Second Coming) needs to be somewhat based on the prior global judgment recorded in Genesis chapters 6–9. I believe God will anoint prophetic ministry that draws and accentuates this parallel between the Genesis flood and the Second Coming of Jesus Christ.

Conclusion

It needs to be reiterated that theistic evolution must be scrutinized by biblical criteria. For the primacy of scripture is the main issue here. I think the five points of this essay, individually and cumulatively, pose an irrefutable case for fiat special creation. The same points are devastating to all three main variant forms of theistic evolution. Good theologians know the theistic version of evolution is pseudobiblical. My challenge to evangelical theistic evolutionists has to do with these five points, nothing more. After monitoring this issue and topic for many years, and having read hundreds of relevant articles and books, I have yet to find one theistic evolutionist who biblically refuted these five points, and in turn, justified theistic evolution. I know I am sounding a bit cocky, but I am so appalled at scholarly and popular theistic evolutionary rhetoric.

Of course, some evangelical theistic evolutionists, in response to this challenge, will find it hard not to wade into scientific criteria. This only goes to show that theistic evolutionists take their cues from naturalistic dogma more than the inscripturated Word of God. But my challenge does not have to do with scientific criteria. Granted, I am convinced that good philosophers of science know that evolution science is pseudoscientific, but that is another huge topic in itself, albeit important. Suffice it to say that evangelical Christians who believe in theistic evolution have been fallaciously intimidated by the tyranny of philosophical naturalism.

A few additional comments are in order concerning theistic evolution proper, progressive creation, and the gap theory. Regarding theistic evolution proper, a main conceptual problem (apart from its biblical problems) is its vagueness about the roles of God and natural selection, and their respective responsibilities for the universe's design and purpose. Regarding progressive creation, there seems to be a resurgence of it among some evangelicals, this theory being akin to the so-called day-age theory. This resurgence is undoubtedly due to the vagueness and scriptural vacuity of theistic evolution proper, on the one hand, and the perceived scientific naivety and scriptural hyperliteralism associated with fiat special creation, on the other hand. Progressive creation seems to be a plausible compromise. Nevertheless, to insist that progressive creation is not a variant form of theistic evolution, as some evangelicals do, is naive at best, and deceptive at worst. This insistence is an expedient semantical ploy, as progressive creation essentially means naturalistic evolution over eons of time, with some periodic divine fiat creations. In a nutshell, progressive creation (a) definitely does injustice to the biblical record, (b) does not accord well with the philosophical bias (inherent in consistent evolutionism) against the divine element, and (c) is a hypothesis, the case of which is empirically dubious.

Regarding the gap theory, several scriptural problems can be briefly highlighted. The positing of two separate creation sets (one before and one after the gap), the pre-Adamic creation scenario (whereby there are living physical creatures prior to Gen. 1:3), the insertion of the geological ages between Genesis 1:1 and 1:2, the early earth ruination scenario (whereby Gen. 1:2 is believed to describe the earth after a great cataclysm altered the earth's previous condition), and the interpretation of the Hebrew word *hayetha* in Genesis 1:2 to mean "became" (instead of the usual "was" rendering), are all theologically expedient and lacking support in the remainder of Genesis and the Bible as a whole. Thus the gap theory says there was physical suffering and death of animals (i.e., dinosaurs) during the geological ages before the fall of Adam, and before the fall of Lucifer/Satan. So the question arises as to who or what is ultimately responsible for the suffering and death of these (pre-Adamic) animals. You do not hear much about the gap theory anymore, and for good reason. But myriads of Christians have believed this theory since Thomas Chalmers, a Scottish theologian, popularized it in the early 1800s.

I would now like to exhort the evangelical community. First, we obviously need to be more discerning regarding our doctrine of creation. On the basis of the five points in this essay, I urge Christians to personally repudiate theistic evolution in all its variant forms. I would not go so far as to say it should be given creed status, but I definitely urge Christians to personally adhere to the biblical doctrine of fiat special creation, as defined earlier.

Second, we need to be courageous and bold, for there has been a glaring gap of ministry among evangelicals on the theological front. Rather than shying away from those inside our faith communities who have adopted unbiblical creation views, we need to lovingly, wisely, staunchly, and articulately challenge them. Foremost, we should be challenging the biblical integrity of theistic evolution (rather than naively glossing over the biblical inconsistencies and subsequent implications). As there will be times when we are misunderstood and ridiculed on the theological front, we must always keep in mind that creation is a work of the Holy Spirit that is spiritually discerned (1 Cor. 2:13f).

Third, we need to think rationally about divine revelation. Foremost, we do God's written Word a great disservice when we fail to underscore and elucidate the theological coherence of fiat special creation. For the beginning chapters of Genesis, the remainder of the Bible, and the climactic evangel message are not incoherent. By neglecting to underscore and elucidate the theological coherence of fiat special creation, we thus deny the rational faculty that God has endowed us with. And make no mistake about it, our rational faculty definitely concurs with the five points of this essay, contrary to the psuedorationality promoted by evangelical theistic evolutionists. Christian scholars are misled by modernist rationalism (not rationality) when they believe theistic evolutionary views are necessary for intellectual and evangelistic credibility. Broadly speaking, a great need in the evangelical church is to cultivate a holistic Christian experience whereby we love God with all our spirit, all our emotions, and all our physical strength, as well as all our minds (Mark 12:30). Astute and discerning Christians understand that belief in fiat special creation is synonymous with loving God with all our minds and, as such, bolsters the broader holistic love for God. Likewise, belief in theistic evolution restricts loving God with all our minds and, as such, subtly stymies, if not fractures, the broader holistic love for God. In summary to this third subpoint, the evangelical church needs to affirm rationality as an integral component of Christian faith.

Fourth, we need to be mindful that what we believe about the past reinforces what we believe in the present. So if we want to see the Word of God confirmed with full, authentic, Holy Spirit power in the present, we need to first affirm the Word and power of God in the past—that is, in creation. Conversely, by downplaying the supernatural power of God in the past, the doctrine of theistic evolution, in effect, fosters a deistic (God does not actively intervene in history) general mind-set regarding the present and future. It is no coincidence that theistic evolutionists usually downplay the supernatural element in their perception of (a) biblical history, and (b) Christian experience. Actually, I cannot think of a more crucial foundational theological topic than the opening chapters of Genesis. The interpretation of the beginning chapters of Genesis not only constitutes a crisis of credibility for the evangelical church, but it may very well be the pivotal topic that sets the course for the evangelical church as it proceeds further into the twenty-first century. Are we evangelical Christians going to affirm the Word and power of God, or are we going to capitulate to (a) a lingering modernist rationalism that is wedded to naturalism and (b) a desultory postmodern ethos that denigrates truth, the meaning of texts, rationality, and historical realities?

Contrary to what many think, what the evangelical church believes about creation is extremely important. For there are some serious, far-reaching implications as to how the beginning chapters of Genesis are interpreted. We have noted how the idea of theistic evolution undermines the authority/reliability of scripture and faith in God's ability/willingness to operate supernaturally throughout world history. Thus the hidden motif of theistic evolution is suspiciously similar to the serpent's scheme in Genesis 3:1 when it said, "Did God really say?" Heresy is a word that is not often used today, but it aptly describes what theistic evolution is. The presence of this heresy in our midst should not completely surprise us, as the

New Testament often warns us of deceptive false doctrines or teachings (e.g., 1 Tim. 1:3, 6:3). What may surprise some is how widespread this false doctrine has infiltrated the evangelical church in general. Furthermore, the fact that creation was a nonissue in the early New Testament church does not mean it is a nonissue in the contemporary evangelical church. Just as the early church had to resist certain false doctrines, which are nonissues in the contemporary church, likewise, the contemporary church has to resist certain false doctrines that were nonissues in the early church. Suffice it to say, (a) there is a vital kinetic relationship between true doctrine and true spirituality (1 Tim. 4:16), and (b) the pragmatic impulse in Canada and the United States has, too often, distorted the appreciation of sound (evangelical) doctrine.

Undoubtedly, the current schizophrenic approach to creation is contributing to the anemic state of parts of the evangelical church. Consequently, I do not think we will ever be the dynamic church God wants us to be unless we get our doctrinal house in order. I think it is deplorable how (evangelical) theistic evolutionists sidestep the five main points of this essay. Again, these points warrant repeating.

1. The primary means or repository of divine revelation is the inspired, written Word of God (i.e., the Bible), not nature (i.e., creation).

2. A historical-grammatical study of the Old Testament words yom (day) and yamim (days) supports fiat special creation, not evolutionary creation in any sense.

3. The book of Genesis depicts historical continuity, not nonhistorical prose or mythology.

4. The book of Genesis, and the Bible as a whole, describes a finished, stable, and tainted creation, not a continuous, dynamic, and progressive (evolutionary) creation.

5. The Noahic flood was global, not regional (thus the full geological implications of such a massive catastrophic event must be appreciated, not depreciated).

Long after this essay is considered dated, these five points will indelibly remain. Despite the imperfect and limited accompanying commentary, the five points are, nevertheless, irrefutable. Evangelical Christians ought to be holding their leaders, scholars, and faith communities more accountable regarding these points. The bottom line of this topic and issue is (a) it was a given postulate to the writers and believing characters of the Old and New Testaments that God created the physical order in six/seven literal days as depicted in the book of Genesis, and (b) the five points of this essay cannot be erased from the written Word of God and the consciousness of God's people.

In conclusion, I am reminded of a conversation I had concerning this essay with an influential person in the evangelical Christian media. The first question this person asked me was, "What are your scientific credentials?" Once again, my heart sank, for the question typified the misconceived mind-set of far too many evangelical Christians, who fail to understand that the crux of this topic and issue does not have to do with science or credentials. Rather the crux of this topic and issue has to do with the Bible and its contents. Not only are one's scientific credentials irrelevant, but so are one's religious credentials, be it a PhD from some well-known seminary or a title from some denominational organization. The reason I am somewhat critical of what I call "credentialism" is that most people who highlight their (scientific or religious) credentials have the mind-set of a "scholar" rather than a "thinker."

In his book *The Christian Mind* (South Bend, IN: Servant Publications, 1963), Harry Blamires, the English Christian apologist, made this distinction: scholars essentially record, describe, are tentative, and conform to the status quo, while thinkers, on the other hand, go beyond the scholarly mandate and dissect, discern, arrive at definite conclusions, and advocate original decisive action. Our culture has many scholars, but relatively few thinkers. Rather than being a long scholarly document, this essay was written to stir evangelical Christians to be thinkers. You do not necessarily need to know a lot about science, nor do you need to have any credentials per se, to thoughtfully conclude that "God did not use evolution." All you need is to be a serious student of God's inscripturated Word and endeavor to love God with all your mind.

Whereas I do not believe the thesis of this essay is unfathomably complicated, the concept of divine creation, admittedly, can get complicated (to say the least). We thus need to remember that, if God's acts of creation could be fully understood by the human mind, God would be no greater than that mind. The elements of humility and faith are intrinsic to the doctrine of creation. Nonetheless, the five-point thesis (and challenge) of this essay still demands a biblical and thoughtful response from all evangelical Christians adhering to theistic evolution. Will they address the challenge? Can they refute the challenge? Some evangelical theistic evolutionists may attempt to address the challenge, but I do not think any will succeed in refuting it.

Ephesians 4:11–15 reads: "It was he who gave some to be apostles, some to be prophets, some to be evangelists, and some to be pastors and teachers, to prepare God's people for works of service, so that the body of Christ may be built up until we all reach unity in the faith, and in the knowledge of the Son of God and become mature, attaining to the whole measure of the fullness of Christ. Then we will no longer be infants, tossed back and forth by the waves, and blown here and there by every wind of teaching and by the cunning and craftiness of men in their deceitful scheming. Instead, speaking the truth in love, we will in all things grow up in him who is the Head, that is, Christ." As a kind of specialized "teacher," in accordance with the above scripture, I submit this essay and challenge to the evangelical community.

Printed in the United States
By Bookmasters